D0898401

Getting Ready for Sunday's Sermon:
A Practical Guide for Sermon Preparation

Getting Ready for Sunday's Sermon

A
Practical Guide for Sermon Preparation

Martin Thielen

Broadman Press
Nashville, Tennessee

All Scripture references are from the Revised Standard
Version of the Bible, copyrighted 1946, 1952, © 1971,
1973.

**Library of Congress Cataloging-in-Publication
Data**

Thielen, Martin, 1956-
    Getting ready for Sunday's sermon : a practical guide
for sermon preparation / Martin Thielen.
        p. cm.
    ISBN 0-8054-2121-1
    1. Preaching. 2.Sermons--Outlines, syllabi, etc. 3.
Homiletical illustrations. I. Title.
BV4211.2 T48 1990
251' .01--dc20

                                            89-34344
                                              CIP

To Jonathan and Laura

PREFACE

Like most preachers, I preach every Sunday morning. Like many preachers, however, I also preach on Sunday and Wednesday evenings. Sometimes I feel like a sermon factory—producing one, two, even three or more sermons per week, week after week, year after year. I can relate to the pastor who went to visit in the home of one of his church members. A little girl answered the door. "Mama, come quick," she said. "The sermon is here."

I love to preach. Most preachers feel the same way. Producing quality sermons on a consistent basis, however, is hard work. To do it effectively, at least two things are necessary. First, we preachers need some basic principles which guide us as we get ready for Sunday's sermon. Second, we need an arsenal of sermon ideas. *Getting Ready for Sunday's Sermon* addresses these two issues. It outlines six important principles of sermon preparation and contains hundreds of sermon ideas.

Like my previous book, *Getting Ready for Sunday, Getting Ready for Sunday's Sermon* is pragmatic. This is not a book on the theory of preaching, the history of preaching, or even about sermon delivery. It is simply one preacher's method of getting ready for Sunday's sermon, combined with sermon ideas, illustrations, outlines, sermon series possibilities, and other sermonic materials. If you are like me, however, such practical ideas are exactly what you're looking for. If so, this book should prove beneficial to you.

In the following pages I will share six principles which guide me as I get ready for Sunday's sermon:the acrostic, P-R-E-A-C-H. I strive to make my preaching **planned, relevant, engaging, authoritative, comprehensive,** and **human.** Perhaps these principles, along with the many examples, will help you as you get ready for Sunday's sermon.

CONTENTS

1. Planned Preaching   11
2. Relevant Preaching   37
3. Engaging Preaching   60
4. Authoritative Preaching   103
5. Comprehensive Preaching   123
6. Human Preaching   147
   Conclusion   160

1 Planned Preaching

R
E
A
C
H

I graduated from seminary on May 22 and began my first pastorate on June 1. By the end of June, I had exhausted my entire arsenal of old sermons. I decided to put together a preaching calendar for the rest of the year, July through December—26 Sundays. As I stared at that blank calendar, an overwhelming sense of panic gripped me.

I now plan my preaching a year at a time. The problem these days isn't having too many Sundays but having too few. Planned preaching takes away the worry of what to preach on Sunday and makes my preaching more enjoyable and effective.

Why Plan?

Planned preaching offers numerous benefits for a busy pastor. I'll highlight some of the most important in this section.

Planned Preaching Relieves Anxiety

Pastors have enough stressors without constantly worrying about what they are going to preach on Sunday. Half the battle in getting ready for Sunday's sermon is knowing the subject.

My family and I returned from vacation late last

Saturday night. On the way home we passed a church. A light was on in the pastor's office and a lone car was in the parking lot. Inside, some poor pastor was desperately trying to get ready for the next morning's sermon. There is a better way!

Planned preaching helps relieve anxiety in at least two concrete ways. First, when we come to our office on Monday morning, we will know exactly what we're going to preach on next Sunday. We don't have to worry about choosing our subject. Second, since we know our subject, we can begin working on it early in the week. If unexpected interruptions occur during the week, we'll already have the bulk of our sermon completed.

William Barclay once said, "When I was a parish minister, I never wrote a sermon after Thursday."[1] An incident I experienced last week illustrates the wisdom of Barclay's method. On Wednesday afternoon one of our church members died. The funeral was on Friday. On Thursday morning another person died, and the funeral was scheduled for Saturday. Wednesday through Saturday was totally consumed. Fortunately, I had completed my sermon on Wednesday morning. If not, I would have been in trouble on Sunday.

Maybe it doesn't bother you to wonder all week what you'll preach on Sunday. Perhaps you never have unexpected interruptions during the week. If not, planned preaching may not relieve much anxiety for you. But if so, you'll discover that planned preaching can help reduce stress in your ministry.

Planned Preaching Saves Time

The other night I watched a juggler perform on television. *That's a picture of the pastorate,* I thought to myself. Pastors are like jugglers. We constantly juggle three duties of pastoral ministry. First, we provide leadership for our church. We try to lead our church to accomplish its God-given mission. That takes a lot of time. Second, we provide loving, pastoral care for the people in our congregation. Many hours a week are involved in providing such care. And third, we proclaim the gospel through evangelism, worship leadership, and preaching. That also takes a tremendous investment of time. Planned preaching can help us save much of our limited time.

I'm not a serious fisherman, but a few times I've been with those who are. Last year I went fishing with such a man. He knew every part of the lake. We rode in the boat for a long time. I was getting impatient. "Where are we going?" I finally asked.

"We're going where the fish are," he replied.

This man knew where to fish. He didn't waste time fishing in nonproductive areas of the lake. The result was a fine catch of fish and an excellent dinner.

Preachers need to be like this fisherman. We should not waste time in nonproductive sermon preparation. If we don't know what we are preaching on Sunday, we'll waste many hours fishing around for an idea. If we plan our preaching, however, no time will be wasted. We'll know where the fish are, so to speak. We will go straight to Sunday's text. We'll know exactly what kind of illustrations are needed. The time allotted to sermon preparation that week will be well used.

I remember somebody saying that a preacher should spend one hour in the study for every minute in the pulpit. If you are a pastor, you know that's crazy! Nobody has that kind of time, especially if you're preaching Sunday evening and Wednesday night. We must make our limited study time count, and planned preaching will help.

Planned Preaching Allows Time to Gather Supporting Material

For me this is the most important benefit of planned preaching. Having supporting materials means we don't have to start our sermon each week from scratch.

Last year I preached a sermon series on the Ten Commandments. It was among the most enjoyable preaching I've ever done. The reason is clear—I had a tremendous amount of supporting materials. I knew I was going to preach this series for almost a year. By the time I began the series, I had several folders chock-full of illustrations, sermons, and exegetical notes to support the sermons.

I just completed a series of sermons on parenting as part of our Christian Home Emphasis Month. I'd been collecting supporting materials, however, for about seven months. The result was a sermon series I felt good about and which was well received by my congregation.

I have an entire file cabinet dedicated to sermon ideas and their supporting materials. In the cabinet are many files—some for individual sermons, some for sermon series. Whenever I get an idea for a sermon or a series of sermons, I make a file. This filing system is the heart of my planned preaching schedule. Ideas come from personal experiences, Bible reading, general reading, other preachers' sermons, and various other preaching resources. When I get a good idea for a sermon, I jot it down and make a file. I don't do this for vague ideas, they go into a general file which I occasionally look over when I'm desperate for new ideas. Individual files are reserved only for ideas which I think have real possibility. Over the course of several weeks or even several years, I drop supporting materials into these files. For example, for several months I've been collecting material for a Father's Day sermon. My text will be, "Husbands, love your wives as Christ loved the church." The sermon's theme is that the best gift fathers can give their children is a good marriage. I now have numerous supporting materials in the file including several strong illustrations. When Father's Day arrives, I have many raw materials to construct the sermon.

I'm presently collecting materials for a sermon series on the Lord's Prayer and the 23rd Psalm. I'm looking forward to preaching on these beloved passages of Holy Scripture. I'll preach these two series next year—one in the spring and one in the fall. The files for these series already have a good supply of articles, illustrations, exegetical notes, sermons, and notes I've jotted down concerning these two passages of Scripture.

Although gathering supporting materials takes time and effort, the benefits are tremendous. I now have hundreds of solid sermon ideas in my file cabinet. Although I recently moved to a new church and have lots of old sermons I could use, I'm too interested in new ideas to rely heavily on old material.

Having supporting materials allows me to pick the best resources for my sermons rather than just the ones I'm able to scrounge up that particular week. When I get ready for Sunday's sermon, I can choose from many possible resources. This allows me the luxury of choosing only the best illustrations, insights, and exegetical comments.

Sometimes I'm inspired to preach a sermon for which I've not collected any supporting material—a new idea, a special insight, or a pressing need. Those sermons often turn out fine. Consistently, however, my best preaching is the result of having collected numerous supporting materials.

Planned Preaching Produces Better Worship Services

A few years ago, I preached a revival at another church. Several months before the revival I talked to the pastor about the needs of the church and then planned my sermons for the revival. I sent the sermon texts and topics to the person who would be leading music during the revival. A week later I received a curious letter. This music minister was grateful for my information. It allowed him to plan complementary music for the revival. But he was also amazed. He acted as though this kind of cooperation was an unusual event. Unfortunately, it is for many churches.

When we give advance sermon themes to the people responsible for music, a marked improvement in worship can result. When the music minister knows the theme of the service, he or she can intelligently choose hymns, anthems, solos, and other complementary music. Our music minister knows the direction and theme of our worship services at least three months in advance. This allows him, the choir, and me to be partners in worship. It greatly improves the quality of our worship services. The end result is carefully crafted worship services which honor God and meet the needs of people.

Planned Preaching Promotes a Balanced Program of Proclamation

Like many pastors, I plan my preaching a year in advance. The plan is tentative and not always specific. I plan a year in advance only in broad strokes. But the benefit of this approach is the ability to get a bird's-eye view of the year. I ask myself: "Is this a balanced preaching schedule? Have I omitted anything? Have I gone overboard on a particular subject?" Through this kind of planning I'm able to achieve better balance in my preaching. This will be discussed at length in a later chapter.

Planned Preaching Supports the Overall Ministry of the Church

Planned preaching can help you coordinate your preaching schedule with the goals of your church. If, for example, your church is planning a revival, you can schedule a sermon (or sermons) to help prepare for that important emphasis. If your church is going to have a stewardship campaign, you can plan complementary sermons. Perhaps your church is planning a major emphasis on the Sunday School. Scheduling a sermon on the importance of Christian education can do much to enrich that event. By coordinating your annual preaching schedule with your church's plans and goals for the year, you'll help support the entire ministry of your church.

Planned Preaching Encourages Prayerful Sermon Planning and Spirit-Led Preaching

Some preachers feel that planned preaching hampers the work of the Holy Spirit. While I understand that view, the exact opposite is true for me. Much prayer is invested in my preaching plan. I earnestly seek God's leadership as I schedule sermons. My quiet times of sermon preparation and planning are deeply spiritual experiences. God's presence is very much alive in this process.

Planned preaching is a dynamic experience of human

effort and spiritual guidance. If planning is done in the context of prayer and seeking God's will, the result will be Spirit-led preaching which changes the lives of both pastor and congregation. Planned preaching does not hamper God's Spirit. Rather, it offers a unique opportunity for the Holy Spirit to be intimately involved in the planning and the proclamation of the gospel.

How to Plan

Before outlining a specific method for planning your preaching, some initial remarks need to be mentioned. First, planned preaching must be tentative. A preaching schedule should be filled in with a pencil and not a pen. Many times you will need to alter your plan. Last October I had a stewardship sermon scheduled. The Wednesday before I was to preach that sermon an 18-year-old boy from our youth group was tragically killed in an automobile accident. To stay on my preaching schedule that week would have been totally inappropriate. Other factors will also change your schedule—an illness, for example, or a major national or local event which needs to be addressed. Planned preaching should never take away spontaneity. A preaching plan is only that—a plan. It should never become your master.

Second, how far in advance should you plan? Only you can answer. For some it may only be a month, three months, or perhaps six months. As mentioned earlier, I like to plan my preaching a year in advance. When I plan that far in advance, however, I'm only talking about broad strokes. The details are not yet completed. I know what direction I'm going but not what specific road I'll take. I'll know that I'm planning a sermon series on the 23rd Psalm but will not know the specific direction of each sermon or which illustrations I will use. I don't do that until I begin to make specific preparation.

Annual planning is my method. It isn't necessarily the best method. It may not fit your personality or ministry style. Perhaps a three- month planning schedule will work best for you. The overall principle, however, is sound. Planned preaching is important. It will make your preaching better. Try it and find out!

Now let me introduce you to my particular method of annual planning. I use seven sources for planning my preaching—relying heavily upon the calendar. My seven sources are (1) The Christian calendar, (2) the secular calendar, (3) the church calendar, (4) the denominational calendar, (5) my personal calendar, (6) sermon series, and (7) miscellaneous and spontaneous sermons.

The Christian Calendar

The Christian calendar offers much potential for sermon planning. You can choose from such days and seasons as Advent, Christmastide, Epiphany, Lent, Holy Week, Easter, Ascension Sunday, Pentecost Sunday, and Trinity Sunday.

How you use the Christian calendar will depend partly on your denominational heritage. Generally speaking, my denomination pays little attention to the Christian calendar. As of yet, I'm not comfortable following every season and day of the Christian year. At a minimum, however, I observe the four Sundays of Advent (preparation and celebration of Christmas), Holy Week, and Easter. That fills in at least six Sundays of my preaching calendar per year. I go to my sermon idea file which was mentioned earlier, look for sermon ideas which fit these Sundays, and begin to fill in the schedule. For Advent I'm planning a four-week series on the characters of the nativity called "The Manger People." I'll have a sermon based on Mary and Joseph, the shepherds, Jesus, and the Wise Men. For Palm/Passion Sunday I'm planning to focus on the death of Christ and observe the Lord's Supper. My sermon will be called, "The Crucified God." For Easter, I'm planning a sermon from Matthew 28:1-10. I'll call it "A Walk to the Cemetery." To see what my schedule looks like after using the Christian calendar, see the sample Christian calendar at the end of the chapter.

The Secular Calendar

Although I don't feel obligated to follow it, the secular calendar offers an opportunity to preach on significant subjects such as the Christian family (Mother's Day and Father's Day), work (Labor Day), grief (Memorial Day), Christian citizenship (Independence Day), gratitude (Thanksgiving), and new beginnings (New Year's Day). Since people are already thinking about these subjects on these days, they tend to be more receptive to sermons about them.

After choosing which days to follow on the secular calendar, I look through my idea file for appropriate sermons. If at all possible, I schedule a specific sermon. At this point it's probably just an idea, a working title, and a text. If I'm lucky, the file will have one or two illustrations or maybe a sermon by somebody else on the same subject or text. If I don't have any specific ideas, I just fill in the theme for the day—Father's Day, Thanksgiving, or whatever. During the next few weeks or months I'll be on the lookout for a good idea and will file it when I find one.

This year's schedule will have seven sermons based on the secular calendar: a sermon on new beginnings for

New Year's Day, two on the Christian home for Mother's Day and Father's Day, one on freedom for Independence Day, another on the importance of work on Labor Day, a sermon on grief for Memorial Day, and a final one on the spirit of gratitude for Thanksgiving. The dates and titles follow. My preaching schedule now has 13 weeks scheduled.

To see what my preaching schedule looks like with the secular calendar included, see the secular calendar at the end of this chapter.

The Denominational Calendar

Most denominations have several special days during the year. Mine has multitudes of special days—World Hunger Day, Day of Prayer for World Peace, Race Relations Day, Senior Adult Day, Single Adult Day, Sanctity of Life Sunday, Witness Commitment Day, Baptist Men's Day, Cooperative Program Day, Baptist World Alliance Day, Volunteers in Missions Day, Start-a-Church Day, and the list goes on and on. We even have an Annuity Board Sunday. A great opportunity to talk about that salary increase you want!

Obviously, no pastor could, or would even want to observe all these days each year. I simply choose the ones I feel are most important to me and my church. I also tend to choose days for which I already have a good sermon idea! The days chosen will change year by year. One year I may observe Sanctity of Life Sunday, the next year something different.

For this year's preaching schedule I've chosen six denominational Sundays: (1) Witness Commitment Day will be a good challenge to our people to become more concerned about sharing Christ with our community. (2) Baptist Men's Day. It has become a tradition at my church to have a service led by laymen on this day. It's always a good service. (3) Senior Adult Day provides an opportunity to affirm and challenge our many elderly church members.

I have also chosen three other denominational Sundays to focus attention on crucial issues of our time. These include, (4) Day of Prayer for World Peace, (5) World Hunger Day, and (6) Race Relations Day.

My preaching calendar now has 19 sermons scheduled. To see what it looks like, see the sample denominational calendar at the end of the chapter.

The Church Calendar

The events, plans, and goals of our church should also influence our preaching schedule for the year. Examples could include revival preparation, a mission trip, a stewardship campaign, a Gideon speaker (an annual event in my church), at least four Lord's Supper services per year, Sunday School emphasis, missionary emphases, and others.

I'll schedule seven such Sundays next year. They include two Lord's Supper services (two others already fall on days from other calendars—Palm/Passion Sunday and Thanksgiving), a Sunday dedicated to revival preparation, the revival itself, a service in honor of our graduating seniors, a Gideon speaker, and a stewardship sermon as we promote our new budget.

At this point, 26 Sundays have been scheduled—one half of the year. To see my preaching schedule with church calendar events added, please see the church calendar at the end of the chapter.

My Personal Calendar

Like all pastors, I will be out of town several weeks each

year. This next year has at least four such Sundays. Two for vacation, one for a revival I will be preaching at another church, and another for a week of continuing education at a seminary. These weeks are blocked off on the preaching calendar at the end of the chapter.

Sermon Series

My favorite preaching is done in series. These range from a simple two-week series all the way to a ten-week series on the Ten Commandments. A three or four-week series is my favorite length. Ideas for sermon series will appear later in this book. But I block out at least two or three such series per year. Since I know what the subjects will be long in advance, I usually have a lot of supporting materials. This year I have planned three series—a short, three-week series from several passages in the Book of Job; a five-week series on the 23rd Psalm, and a five-week series on the Lord's Prayer.

Although I usually schedule a sermon series back to back, I sometimes have to spread them out. For example, I may spread out a four-week series over a period of five or six Sundays. A special event or holiday may break the series up for a week or two. Since each sermon must stand on its own, that is no real problem.

In some cases I purposely break up the series. For example, if done creatively, the Ten Commandments can still be an effective sermon series. But 10 weeks back to back is a bit much. When I did this series, I scheduled several breaks along the way. It took 16 weeks to conclude the 10 sermons in the series.

After choosing which series to preach for the year, I schedule them on the calendar where they best fit. To see how this fits in with the rest of my preaching schedule, see the sermon series calendar at the end of the chapter.

Miscellaneous and Spontaneous Sermons

You'll not want to fill in every week with the above six sources. Leave some Sundays open for miscellaneous sermons and for spontaneous inspirations. On several Sundays each year you'll need to drop the scheduled plan and go with a sudden inspiration.

By the time I get to this seventh source for annual planning, I already have about 40 sermons scheduled. I now look in the idea file for what I consider to be my best miscellaneous sermons and scatter them throughout the year. Like the entire schedule, these are subject to change, but I like to schedule at least a tentative date.

By the time this process has concluded, I usually have a few blank Sundays left—but not many. I simply leave them blank. Either something will come spontaneously, or else I'll get something out of my idea file when the time comes.

After all this has been done, I now have a final schedule. To show you how this works, please see the final calendar.

One last issue needs to be raised concerning planned preaching. When should you do the planning? Every preacher must come up with his own schedule. A few rare preachers can do it all at once, on a week's retreat or something. That simply doesn't work for me.

I begin working on my annual preaching calendar the summer before the new year begins. I don't have a set time of concentrated effort. I just work on it when I get some spare time. By November I'm usually finished with at least an overview of the new year. To be sure, all the details are not in place. I may know that I'll preach a stewardship sermon on the first Sunday of October, but I may not have any idea what it will be. That's OK; I'll have almost a year to find at least one good idea.

The year is now planned, files are made, and supporting materials are being added regularly. But the actual writing of my sermon is done the week it is preached. I find it impossible to write next month's or even next week's sermon this week. As our Lord once said, "Let the day's own trouble be sufficient for the day"(Matt. 6:34).

I have limited this discussion to Sunday morning sermons. That's where I do the majority of my planning. I also plan for Sunday and Wednesday nights but not nearly as much. I simply do a verse-by-verse Bible study on Wednesday nights after our prayer time and usually stay in some kind of series on Sunday night. The environment is far more relaxed during the evening services, and I often encourage the congregation to dialogue with me about the text. Some pastors manage to write out their Sunday and Wednesday evening messages; I don't even try. I simply take handwritten notes and hope that if I ever use them again I'll remember what I was trying to say!

My sermon preparation begins then by planning ahead. That's the first principle for getting ready for Sunday's sermon. But that's just the beginning. Let's now move to the second principle.

Note

1.William Barclay, *A Spiritual Autobiography* (Grand Rapids: Eerdmans Publishing Co., 1977), . 29.

PREACHING SCHEDULE:
THE CHRISTIAN CALENDAR

Date	Sermon	Date	Sermon
Jan. 3		July 3	
10		10	
17		17	
24		24	
31		31	
Feb. 7		Aug. 7	
14		14	
21		21	
28		28	
Mar. 6		Sept. 4	
13		11	
20		18	
27:	Palm/Passion: The Crucified God	25	
Apr. 3:	Easter: A Walk to the Cemetery	Oct. 2	
10		9	
17		16	
24		23	
May 1		30	
8		Nov. 6	
15		13	
22		20	
29		27	
June 5		Dec. 4:	Advent: "The Manger People" Mary and Joseph
12		11:	Shepherds
19		18:	Christ Child
26		25:	The Wise Men

PREACHING SCHEDULE:
THE SECULAR CALENDAR

Date		Sermon	Date		Sermon
Jan.	3:	New Year's: To Dream Again	July	3:	Independence Day: Let Freedom Ring!
	10			10	
	17			17	
	24			24	
	31			31	
Feb.	7		Aug.	7	
	14			14	
	21			21	
	28			28	
Mar.	6		Sept.	4:	Labor Day: On the Job
	13			11	
	20			18	
	27:	Palm/Passion: The Crucified God		25	
Apr.	3:	Easter: A Walk to the Cemetery	Oct.	2	
	10			9	
	17			16	
	24			23	
May	1			30	
	8:	Mother's Day: Best Supporting Actress	Nov.	6	
	15			13	
	22	Known by His Gratitude		20:	Thanksgiving:
	29:	Memorial Day: Good Grief		27	
June	5		Dec.	4:	Advent: "The Manger People" Mary and Joseph
	12			11:	Shepherds
	19:	Father's Day:		18:	Christ Child

What Children Need from Their Fathers	
26	25: The Wise Men

PREACHING SCHEDULE:
THE DENOMINATIONAL CALENDAR

Date		Sermon	Date		Sermon
Jan.	3:	New Year's: To Dream Again	July	3:	Independence Day: Let Freedom Ring!
	10:	Witness Commitment Day: Making Friends for Christ		10	
	17			17	
	24:	Baptist Men's Day: Men will lead service		24	
	31			31	
Feb.	7		Aug.	7:	Day of Prayer for World Peace: The Tent Is on Fire!
	14:	Race Relations Day: A House Divided		14	
	21			21	
	28			28	
Mar.	6		Sept.	4:	Labor Day: On the Job
	13			11	
	20			18	
	27:	Palm/Passion: The Crucified God		25	
Apr.	3:	Easter: A Walk to the Cemetery	Oct.	2	
	10			9:	World Hunger Day: Give Them

					Something to Eat
	17			16	
	24			23	
May	1:	Senior Adult Day: No Retirement!		30	
	8:	Mother's Day: Best Supporting Actress	Nov.	6	
	15			13	
	22			20:	Thanksgiving:
	29:	Memorial Day: Good Grief		27	
June	5		Dec.	4:	Advent: "The Manger People" Mary and Joseph
	12			11:	Shepherds
	19:	Father's Day: What Children Need from Their Fathers		18:	Christ Child
	26			25:	The Wise Men

PREACHING SCHEDULE:
THE CHURCH CALENDAR

Date		Sermon	Date		Sermon
Jan.	3:	New Years: To Dream Again	July	3:	Independence Day: Let Freedom Ring!
	10:	Witness Commitment Day: Making Friends for Christ		10	
	17			17	
	24:	Baptist Men's Day: Men will lead service		24	
	31			31	
Feb.	7:	Gideon Speaker	Aug.	7:	Day of Prayer for World Peace: The Tent Is on Fire!

	14:	Race Relations Day: A House Divided		14	
	21			21	
	28			28	
Mar.	6		Sept.	4:	Labor Day: On the Job
	13			11:	Lord's Supper: Remember
	20			18	
	27:	Palm/Passion: The Crucified God		25	
Apr.	3:	Easter: A Walk to the Cemetery	Oct.	2:	Stewardship: Two Copper Coins
	10			9:	World Hunger Day: Give Them Something to Eat
	17:	Revival Preparation: Can Can These Bones Live?		16	
	24:	Revival		23	
May	1:	Senior Adult Day: No Retirement!		30	
	8:	Mother's Day: Best Supporting Actress	Nov.	6	
	15			13	
	22:	Senior Recognition: Sending Them Off		20:	Thanksgiving: Known by His Gratitude
	29:	Memorial Day: Good Grief		27	
June	5		Dec.	4:	Advent: "The Manger People" Mary and Joseph
	12			11:	Shepherds

19: Father's Day:
What
Children Need
from their Fathers   18: Christ Child

26: Lord's Supper:
A Package from
Home   25: The Wise Men

PREACHING SCHEDULE:
MY PERSONAL CALENDAR

Date		Sermon	Date		Sermon
Jan.	3:	New Year's: To Dream Again	July	3:	Independence Day: Let Freedom Ring!
	10:	Witness Commitment Day: Making Friends for Christ		10:	Cont. Ed. Gone to Conference. Get supply.
	17			17	
	24:	Baptist Men's Day: Men will lead service		24	
	31			31	
Feb.	7:	Gideon speaker	Aug.	7:	Day of Prayer for World Peace: The Tent Is on Fire!
	14:	Race Relations Day: A House Divided		14	
	21			21	
	28			28	
Mar.	6		Sept.	4:	Labor Day: On the Job
	13			11:	Lord's Supper: Remember
	20			18	
	27:	Palm/Passion: The Crucified God		25	
Apr.	3:	Easter:	Oct.	2:	Stewardship:

	A Walk to the Cemetery			Two Copper Coins
10:	Out for Revival		9:	World Hunger Day: Give Them Something to Eat
17:	Revival Preparation: Can These Bones Live?		16	
24:	Revival		23	
May 1:	Senior Adult Day: No Retirement!		30	
8:	Mother's Day: Best Supporting Actress	Nov.	6	
15			13	
22:	Senior Recognition: Sending Them Off		20:	Thanksgiving: Known by His Gratitude
29:	Memorial Day: Good Grief		27	
June 5:	Vacation!	Dec.	4:	Advent: "The Manger People" Mary and Joseph
12:	Vacation!		11:	Shepherds
19:	Father's Day: What Children Need from Their Fathers		18:	Christ Child
26:	Lord's Supper: A Package from Home		25:	The Wise Men

PREACHING SCHEDULE: SERMON SERIES

Date		Sermon	Date		Sermon
Jan.	3:	New Year's: To Dream Again	July	3:	Independence Day: Let Freedom Ring!
	10:	Witness Commitment Day: Making Friends for Christ		10:	Cont. Ed. Go to conference. Get supply.
	17			17	
	24:	Baptist Men's Day: Men will lead service.		24	
	31			31	
Feb.	7:	Gideon speaker	Aug.	7:	Day of Prayer for World Peace: The Tent Is on Fire!
	14:	Race Relations Day: A House Divided		14:	Job Mini-Series Job's Faith
	21:	Psalm 23 Series		21:	Job's Friends
	28:	Psalm 23 Series		28:	Job's Faults
Mar.	6:	Psalm 23 Series	Sept.	4:	Labor Day: On the Job
	13:	Psalm 23 Series		11:	Lord's Supper: Remember
	20:	Psalm 23 Series		18	
	27:	Palm/Passion: The Crucified God		25	
Apr.	3:	Easter: A Walk to the Cemetery	Oct.	2:	Stewardship: Two Copper Coins
	10:	Out for Revival		9:	World Hunger Day: Give Them Something to Eat
	17:	Revival Preparation: Can These Bones Live?		16:	Lord's Prayer Series
	24:	Revival		23:	Lord's Prayer

May   1: Senior Adult Day:
          No Retirement

       8: Mother's Day:
          Best Supporting
          Actress

      15

      22: Senior Recognition:
          Sending Them Off

      29: Memorial Day:
          Good Grief

June   5: Vacation!

      12: Vacation!
      19: Father's Day:
          What
          Children Need
          from Their Fathers

      26: Lord's Supper:
          A Package from
          Home

          Series
      30: Lord's Prayer
          Series

Nov.   6: Lord's Prayer
          Series

      13: Lord's Prayer
          Series

      20: Thanksgiving:
          Known by His
          Gratitude

      27

Dec.   4: Advent: "The
          Manger People"
          Mary and Joseph

      11: Shepherds

      18: Christ Child

      25: The Wise Men

PREACHING SCHEDULE: MISCELLANEOUS

Date		Sermon	Date		Sermon
Jan.	3:	New Years: To Dream Again	July	3:	Independence Day: Let Freedom Ring!
	10:	Witness Commitment Day: Making Friends for Christ		10:	Cont. Ed. Gone to Conference. Get supply
	17:	Strategies for Surviving Stress		17:	Overcoming Burnout
	24:	Baptist Men's Day: Men will lead service.		24	
	31			31:	Who Is This Man?

Feb.	7:	Gideon speaker	Aug.	7:	Day of Prayer for World Peace: The Tent Is on Fire!
	14:	Race Relations Day: A House Divided		14:	Job Mini-Series Job's Faith
	21:	Psalm 23 Series		21:	Job's Friends
	28:	Psalm 23 Series		28:	Job's Faults
Mar.	6:	Psalm 23 Series	Sept.	4:	Labor Day: On the Job
	13:	Psalm 23 Series		11:	Lord's Supper: Remember
	20:	Psalm 23 Series		18	
	27:	Palm/Passion: The Crucified God		25:	When Life Is Unfair
Apr.	3:	Easter: A Walk to the Cemetery	Oct.	2:	Stewardship: Two Copper Coins
	10:	Out for revival		9:	World Hunger Day: Give Them Something to Eat
	17:	Revival Preparation: Can These Bones Live?		16:	Lord's Prayer Series
	24:	Revival		23:	Lord's Prayer Series
May	1:	Senior Adult Day: No Retirement		30:	Lord's Prayer Series
	8:	Mother's Day: Best Supporting Actress	Nov.	6:	Lord's Prayer Series
	15:	The Secret of Contentment		13:	Lord's Prayer Series
	22:	Senior Recognition: Sending Them Off		20:	Thanksgiving: Known by His

					Gratitude
	29:	Memorial Day: Good Grief		27	
June	5:	Vacation!	Dec.	4:	Advent: "The Manger People" Mary and Joseph
	12:	Vacation!		11:	Shepherds
	19:	Father's Day: What Children Need from Their Fathers		18	Christ Child
	26:	Lord's Supper: A Package from Home		25:	The Wise Men

2 RELEVANT PREACH

A minister's wife told her daughter, "Go to the church and fetch your father for supper."

The girl walked into the back of the sanctuary and saw her father sitting in one of the pews. A moment later he moved to another pew, paused a few minutes, then went to another. This went on for some time. "Daddy," she finally interrupted, "it's time for supper." On the way home she asked about his strange behavior in the church.

"On Saturday evenings," he explained, "I always come to the church and sit where each of our church members sit. I try to imagine how they feel."

If our preaching is going to be heard, it must be relevant to our congregation. We, like the preacher in the old story mentioned above, must sit where they sit and preach to their felt needs. Good preaching speaks to the fears, joys, pains, questions, feelings, struggles, and concerns of our parishioners.

When I stand behind the pulpit to preach, I pause for a moment and look at the congregation. I know what's on their minds. They are asking the same question I ask when I listen to a sermon, *What difference does this make in my life?* They will not ask this question publicly, but they ask it nevertheless.

If we begin our sermon by talking about something

people consider irrelevant to life, such as the architecture of the Temple (I once heard a 40-minute sermon on this inspiring subject!), we've lost them. If, on the other hand, we speak of real, life-and-blood issues, they will hear us.

Henri Nouwen spoke of this kind of preaching in his classic book *The Wounded Healer.* He said:

> Preaching is the careful and sensitive articulation of what is happening in the community so that those who listen can say: "You say what I suspected, you express what I vaguely felt, you bring to the fore what I fearfully kept in the back of my mind. Yes, yes—you say who we are, you recognize our condition."[1]

That kind of connection with people makes preaching relevant and thus effective. Henry Grady Davis put it this way: Preaching

> must be loaded with the realities of the human heart. It must concern the deep and universal questions: life and death, courage and fear, love and hate, trust and doubt, guilt and forgiveness, pain and joy, shame, remorse, compassion, and hope. Only among these can be found a serious answer to the question, "What difference does it make?"[2]

Relevancy is certainly not the only issue in preaching, nor is it the most significant. More important than any other factor is that our sermons be rooted in biblical truth. But if our preaching is to get a hearing, it must first be pertinent. Every sermon begins with this possibility. Frederick Buechner put it well in his book *Telling the Truth.*

> The preacher pulls the little cord that turns on a lectern light and deals out his note cards like a riverboat gambler. The stakes have never been higher. Two minutes from now he may have lost his listeners completely to their own

thoughts, but at this minute he has them in the palm of his hand. The silence in the shabby church is deafening because everybody is listening to it. Everybody is listening including even himself. Everybody knows the kind of things he has told them before and not told them, but who knows what this time, out of the silence, he will tell them?[3]

Whenever we preach, we must keep in mind that our congregation is full of strugglers. When I look out at my congregation and reflect on their pain, I am overwhelmed. When people come to church on Sunday, they need a word from God which speaks to their needs.

In his book *How to Preach to People's Needs*, Edgar Jackson cited a poll that was taken in a large church. The poll illustrates the many needs people have. By averaging the results, Jackson concluded:

In a congregation of five hundred people, it is reasonable to assume that at least one hundred have been so recently bereaved as to feel an acute sense of loss. Probably a third of the married persons are facing problems of personality adjustment that may weaken or destroy their home life. At least half of the five hundred can be assumed to have problems of emotional adjustment in school, work, home, or community that endanger their happiness. Others may have neuroses ranging from alcohol addiction to lesser forms of obsessions and anxiety states. Perhaps fifteen or more are homosexually inclined and another twenty-five depressed. Another hundred may be suffering from so great a feeling of guilt or fear of discovery that their peace of mind and health are jeopardized. The rare individual with complete peace of mind and soul is probably surrounded by those who are carrying several heavy burdens within.[4]

Pastors cannot ignore such issues if they want to be

effective preachers. We must not divorce Sunday from the experiences people have Monday through Saturday. The good news is that this kind of preaching is not difficult. The Bible, our resource book for preaching, is extremely relevant. It's a story of the human drama—a story about people's struggles, joys, and pain. It is a record of God's breaking into the world in meaningful ways.

Universal Relevance

Some topics are universally germane. People are not so different. All of us experience similar emotions, struggles, and joys.

Several years ago an advertising agency was commissioned to discover the ten most pressing needs of people. They were alienation, fear of death, inner emptiness, family turmoil, purposelessness, hopelessness, loneliness, peace of mind, guilt, and lack of self-control.

Although I haven't had much time to reflect on it, this study offers the possibility of some relevant preaching. I'm considering preaching a series on these ten problems or at least on some of them. The series could be called "God's Answers for People's Problems." The overall text could be Philippians 4:19: "My God will supply every need of yours according to his riches in glory in Christ Jesus."

To suggest simplistic answers to these ten major human problems would be shallow. But the Christian faith has much to offer in dealing with these human struggles; the gospel offers many resources for overcoming these problems. Ten sermons could be developed from the above-mentioned study. The basic format would be to illustrate the problem and then move toward some solutions.

God's Answers to People's Problems

1. God's answer for alienation is reconciliation—a major biblical theme. In 2 Corinthians 5:19, Paul said, "God was in Christ, reconciling the world unto himself"(KJV). You could begin the sermon by speaking about the modern experience of alienation. People often feel alienated from God, nature, other people, and even themselves. Many illustrations could be offered. You could then move toward God's solution of reconciliation. God can help us heal broken relationships. Through faith in Christ, we can begin the process of reconciliation.

2. God's answer for inner emptiness is fullness in Christ and abundant living. John 10:10 says, "I came that they may have life, and have it abundantly." You would need to explain that abundant living doesn't mean everything is wonderful and happy. But it does mean that we can experience quality living. When we know and serve God, our life has greater meaning and fullness.

3. God's answers for family turmoil are varied. While no easy answers should be given, our faith does offer some solutions. Having a common faith can help families weather the difficulties of family life. God can offer strength and hope for troubled times. And the Bible offers practical guidance for family relationships (see Eph. 5—6, for example), which, if followed, go a long way toward resolving family turmoil.

4. God's answer for purposelessness is discipleship. Purposelessness is rampant in our nation. Like the popular song said several years ago, many people feel their lives are nothing but dust in the wind.

Christ calls people to follow Him. When we dedicate

ourselves to being His disciples, we have a sense of purpose in our lives. When we join ourselves to a cause bigger than ourselves, we find the solution to purposelessness.

5. God's answer to hopelessness is hope. Many people have no hope. Most ministers have, at some time, counseled these kinds of folks. These people need new hope for living, and hope is a major biblical theme—hope for life and hope for death. God is a God of re-creation and resurrection.

6. God's answer for loneliness is fellowship. Many people today feel lonely. This truth would not be hard to illustrate. Faith offers us the answer of fellowship. We can have relationship with God and also with the community of faith, the church.

7. God's answer for peace of mind is inner peace. We live in an age of anxiety. Faith, however, offers peace which we cannot even explain. As Paul said in Philippians 4:7, "The peace of God, which passes all understanding, will keep your hearts and your minds in Christ Jesus."

8. God's answer for guilt is forgiveness. All have sinned. All experience guilt. The head of one mental hospital said, "I could release half of my patients if I could but find a way to release them from their sense of guilt."

Grace is a central theme, if not the central theme, of the gospel. Forgiveness is available for all. As the psalmist said, "As far as the east is from the west,/ so far does he remove our transgressions from us"(103:12). In the New Testament we read, "If we confess our sins, he is faithful and just, and will forgive our sins and cleanse us from all unrighteousness"(1 John 1:9).

9. God's answer for lack of self-control is spiritual maturity. In Galatians 5:23 we learn that one fruit of the

Spirit is self-control. As we mature in our faith, we can grow in this important area.

10. God's answer for the fear of death is the hope of eternal life. No one is immune from death or the fear of dying, but our faith is in Christ who said, "I am the resurrection and the life; he who believes in me, though he die, yet shall he live"(John 11:25).

I don't know yet what will become of this sermon series idea. I've begun a file on it and will gather supporting materials for a long time. I may end up only preaching on about half the problems. Or I may just preach scattered, individual sermons from it. I may even do some dialogue sermons where I ask people from the congregation to tell how their faith helped them work through some of these problems.

Another example of a universally relevant subject is parenting. The majority of adults in most congregations are parents. Although their children will be different ages, most mothers and fathers want to be effective parents. Sermons on this subject will always be welcomed.

I just completed a three-week series of sermons on parenting. I called it, "Principles for Parenting." The entire series was based on Ephesians 6:4 which says, "Fathers, do not provoke your children to anger, but bring them up in the discipline and instruction of the Lord."

I began the series with the following story. A lady was dragging five children onto a bus. The bus driver asked her, "Are all these children yours, or is this a picnic?"

She replied, "They're all mine, Sir; and it ain't no picnic!"

I acknowledge that parenting is hard work. Our text, however, offers some solid principles to follow in our parenting. I called these the principles of love, limits, and lessons and developed a sermon on each one.

Paul began the verse by saying, "Do not provoke your children to anger." In Colossians 3:21, he added, "lest they become discouraged." Paul commanded parents not to continually put down their children. To do so wounds their self-esteem. Put positively, this can mean, love your children. Affirm them. Build them up; don't tear them down. The entire sermon was built on this principle, and several concrete ways to express parental love were developed.

Paul continued this verse by saying, "Bring them up in . . . discipline." This can be called the principle of limits. This sermon applied only to parents who had children living at home. The issue of fair, consistent, and loving discipline was the subject of the sermon. I began the sermon with the following story which helped capture the attention of the congregation. I heard Wayne Dehoney tell this story in a sermon many years ago.

A woman was cooking a special new recipe for a wonderful dinner. She had worked extremely hard on this meal. Her small son, however, was giving her fits. He kept coming into the kitchen and saying, "Mommy this, Mommy that" and basically driving her crazy. At one point he came tearing through the kitchen and knocked her beautifully prepared dinner all over the floor. In anger she grabbed the poker and started after him. He went running out the door, down the front steps, and under the house as far as he could crawl. She crawled in after him but decided this was an undignified thing for her to do. She decided to let her husband take care of this situation when he got home. When he arrived, she said: "Do something about your son! Go outside and discipline him!" So he crawled under the house, looking all around, until he saw two bright eyes peering around a pillar. A soft voice said, "Paw, is she after you, too?"

Ephesians 6:4 concludes by telling parents to also bring up their children in the "instruction of the Lord." I called this "the principle of lessons." This third and final sermon focused on some of the lessons parents need to be teaching their children—by word and deed.

I preached these sermons to help the families in my congregation. I could take this same series, however, and preach it most anywhere. Parenting is one of many universally relevant topics.

Another such topic is problems. Everyone has problems. I recall the story of the man who had a reputation for extreme brevity. He was asked to give a speech. His topic was problems. He was told that a good speech had three points and a poem. He worked hard on developing three points and a closing poem. The title of his speech was "Problems." His speech follows:

Point number one: I got 'em.

Point number two: You got 'em.

Point number three: We all got 'em.

Closing poem: Adam had 'em.

A relevant sermon on the subject of problems can be found in 1 Kings 14:25-27. It's an obscure passage but has a lot of possibilities. The sermon could be called "When Shishak Comes." The text tells a story about King Rehoboam. In 926 B.C., Shishak, king of Egypt, came against Judah and plundered their treasury. He also took the golden shields which the people used in worship. This was a terrible time for the nation and for Rehoboam. Although Rehoboam was basically a bad king, he did something positive at this point. He rebuilt the golden shields. The gold was all gone so he had to use bronze. But he knew that life and worship must go on, so he compensated for the loss the best he could.

The story has significant lessons. All people, even kings, have problems. Problems are a reality of life. We cannot escape them. Faith does not protect us from adversity. Numerous illustrations could be found for this point.

The major focus of this sermon is Rehoboam's response. He could have responded in many ways, but he chose to make the best of a bad situation. He rebuilt the golden shields. When problems come upon us, we, like Rehoboam, must compensate and go on. The secret of successful living is not avoiding problems; we cannot. The secret is making the best out of a difficult situation and moving on with life. Our faith in God offers us several resources to do just that.

This sermon idea, filled with several interesting illustrations, will get a good hearing anywhere. People face problems every day. When Shishak comes, they, too, need to rebuild the golden shields.

Another universally relevant topic is the search for meaning. People everywhere want to experience a meaningful life. Such was the search of the writer of Ecclesiastes. I recently preached a four-week series on this book called, "The Secret of Life." Although much of the Book of Ecclesiastes is negative and pessimistic, several positive insights can be found. Many of the insights and illustrations for this series came from the profound book by Rabbi Harold Kushner, *When All You've Ever Wanted Isn't Enough.*[5]

Six months ago I was asked to perform a funeral for a man with no church home. I spent a lot of time with his family in preparing for the funeral service. I wanted to know something about this man: What did he do with his life? What were his interests, values, and dreams? After over an hour with the family, however, I still knew almost nothing. Finally his wife actually said, "His main interest in life was watching television."

As far as I could tell, the man knew no meaning in life. He simply existed day by day, watched a lot of TV, and died.

Most people want more out of life. Such was the case of the writer of Ecclesiastes. This book records his search for the secret of life. What follows is an overview of my sermon series on this subject.

The Secret of Life 1: I began the series by looking at some wrong paths for finding a meaningful life. Where had the writer of Ecclesiastes looked for meaning yet been disappointed? The text was 1:16 to 2:11. In this passage we see that the writer of Ecclesiastes traveled down four unsuccessful paths in his quest to discover the secret of life. Each one of these paths was briefly reviewed.

First, Ecclesiastes tried philosophy. In 1:16, we read, "I have acquired great wisdom." Yet wisdom did not satisfy. Ecclesiastes concluded in verse 18, "For in much wisdom is vexation, and he who increases knowledge increases sorrow."

Next, Ecclesiastes tried the path of pleasure. In 2:1 he said, "Come now, I will make a test of pleasure; enjoy yourself." So he indulged in wine (v. 3), women (v. 8), and music (v. 8). Unfortunately, pleasure did not satisfy the deep longing in his heart for meaning. While it's fun for awhile, it can become like a carnival ride which never ends, leaving us dissatisfied and ill.

Next, Ecclesiastes turned to possessions. In verse 7, he said, "I had also great possessions." This is one of the most popular means for seeking the good life. Like wisdom and education, however, possessions will not satisfy the deep longing in our soul for a meaningful life. The problem with possessions is that they never satisfy. Somebody once asked John D. Rockefeller how much money it would take to be really satisfied. He answered, "Just a little bit more." Such is the case with things. We acquire more and more, but contentment remains elusive.

So far, Ecclesiastes tried three paths in his quest for the secret of life—philosophy, pleasure, and possessions. Unfortunately, none satisfied. So he tried a fourth path, the path of production. He tried to find meaning in his career, in his successes and accomplishments. In verse 4, he said, "I made great works."

Production is perhaps the most popular path of all for finding meaning in life. Americans try to find ultimate meaning in work, success, and accomplishments. While our work is extremely important, one can find many examples of people who make it to the top of their field yet still are restless, discontented, and unhappy. Such was the experience of Ecclesiastes. He concluded: "Then I considered all that my hands had done and the toil I had spent in doing it, and behold, all was vanity and a striving after wind" (2:11).

So the writer of Ecclesiastes began by telling us the wrong paths, where not to look for the secret of life. It's like the following story. A man went for a walk in the forest and got lost. He wandered around for hours trying to find his way back to town, trying one path after another, but none of them led out. Then abruptly he came across another hiker walking through the forest. He cried out: "Thank God for another human being. Can you show me the way back to town?" The other man replied: "No, I'm lost too. But we can help each other in this way. We can tell each other which paths we have already tried and been disappointed in. That will help us find the one that leads out."[6]

The second, third, and fourth sermons of this series focused on the right paths: (1) living in the present moment, (2) enjoying relationships with others, and (3), having faith in God.

The Secret of Life 2: Years ago a popular song said, "The secret of life is enjoying the passage of time." That's the point of the second sermon of this series based on Ecclesiastes 9:4-10.

In this passage, the writer of Ecclesiastes said that successful living is to live in the present moment— that this is a vivid way. He spoke about living dogs and dead lions. Although dogs were considered lowly and detestable creatures in ancient days and lions were considered to be noble and great, Ecclesiastes declared that it's better to be a live dog than a dead lion.

People tend to live their lives dwelling on the past or the future. Ecclesiastes reminded us, however, that all we have is today. If we're going to live, we'd better do it now. It's all we have. Tomorrow will be too late. Many illustrations can make this point.

In the text, Ecclesiastes offered several clues as to how we can live in the present moment. In verse 7, he said that we should "eat your bread with enjoyment, and drink your wine with a merry heart." Happiness isn't found in the big events of life as much as in simple pleasures such as eating a meal with your family and friends.

A second way to enjoy the passage of time is to do some celebrating along the way. In verse 8, Ecclesiastes spoke of wearing white garments and putting oil on our heads. These are images of festivity and celebration.

An 85-year-old woman from the hills of Kentucky was

once asked what she would do if she could live her life over again. She said she would "eat more ice cream and less beans."[7]

A famous essay by Robert Hastings from his Broadman book *Tinyburg Tales* called "The Station" concludes with these words:

> So stop pacing the aisles and counting the miles and peering ahead. Instead, swim more rivers, climb more mountains, kiss more babies, count more stars. Go barefoot oftener. Ride more merry-go-rounds, eat more ice cream, watch more sunsets. Life must be lived as we go along. The station will come soon enough.[8]

A third way to live life fully in the present moment is to enjoy relationships with others. In verse 9, Ecclesiastes told his readers to "enjoy life with the wife whom you love." But you had better do it now. Tomorrow may be too late.

A play on television several years ago featured a young man and woman standing at the railing of an ocean liner. They had just gotten married, and this cruise was their honeymoon. They were talking about how much their love and marriage meant to them, far beyond their expectations. The young man said, "If I were to die tomorrow, I would feel that my life had been full because I have known your love." His bride replied, "Yes, I feel the same way." They kissed and moved away from the rail, and the audience could now see the name of their ship on a life preserver: *The Titanic*.[9]

Finally, the writer of Ecclesiastes urged us to enjoy the passage of time by throwing ourselves into our work and activities. In verse 10, he said, "Whatever your hand finds to do, do it with all your might."

Getting caught up in all the complexities of life and

missing the obvious is easy. One of the great secrets of life is living in the present moment, enjoying the passage of time.

The Secret of Life 3: The text for this sermon is Ecclesiastes 4:7-11. Because this is the easiest sermon to prepare, I'll not give a detailed overview. The theme of the sermon is that meaningful life is found only in relationships. "Two are better than one"(v. 9), declared the writer of Ecclesiastes. In this context he was not talking about marriage. The text is broader than that. It speaks of relationships in general. A sermon on our need for others and the benefits of relationships can easily be developed from this text. A strong word can be said about the importance of being part of the community of faith in a local church.

The Secret of Life 4: The final sermon of this series deals with the subject of faith. Ultimately, the secret of life is found in relationship with God. I began this sermon by briefly reviewing the previous three sermons, by recounting the pilgrimage we had started three weeks ago.

I then turned to the final text, Ecclesiastes 12:1-7 and 13. In the final words of the book, the writer of Ecclesiastes said, "Remember also your creator" (v.1). Ultimately, the secret of life is faith. Life will bring joy and pain, life and death. Our only real security is faith in God.

A small boy once asked his father what holds up the world. The father replied that the world rests upon the back of a large turtle. The answer sufficed for a day or two, but the son returned and asked again what held up the turtle. The turtle, said the father, rests upon the back of a large tiger. In time the boy wanted to know what held up the tiger. The father, panicking a bit at the direction this was going, told his son that the tiger rested upon the back of a large elephant. Inevitably, the question arose, "What holds up the elephant?" The father, thoroughly exasperated, said, "Son, it's elephants all the way down!"[10]

What are the elephants upon which we stand? This was the question behind my final sermon. I wanted us to think about the foundations of life. Ecclesiastes told us that we need to rest upon the foundation of faith.

The remainder of the sermon explored our need for faith for life and also for death. In life we need faith to find meaning, direction, values, and strength for living. In death we need faith to give us hope for eternal life. Several illustrations were given to support this theme. I closed with a discussion I'd recently had with a woman of faith who was also a cancer patient.

She didn't pretend that everything was fine. She hurt and she was scared. She wanted to live. But she knew that in life or death her faith would sustain her. She looked at me and said something I'll never forget. "Either way," she said, "live or die, with faith, you win."

The above are just a few examples of sermons based on subjects which are universally pertinent such as problems, parenting, or our search for meaning. Much of our preaching, however, needs to be relevant on a more specific level. To that I now turn our attention.

Local Relevance

Although some topics are universally germane, many of the needs among our congregation are localized and specific. As Fred Craddock pointed out: "Paul never wrote: 'To whom it may concern: Here are some views on the slavery issue.' He did write: 'Dear Philemon: Let's talk about Onesimus.'"[11]

Good preaching must be done in the context of specific ministry. To be relevant, it must address the unique concerns of a specific congregation. To quote Craddock again:

> When I preached in my church, I had buried the dead, I had married the young, I had counseled, I had been in the hospital. If a person is a good pastor, he does an exegesis of the congregation as well as of the text. He can close his eyes and tell you where the people sit on Sunday morning. Even a mediocre sermon to people who love you is great.
>
> People say to me, "You must come hear our minister. He's marvelous." So I go, and when I hear him preach, homiletically it's perhaps a C+. But to their ears it's A+ because he had the wedding, the funeral, the crisis counseling. In that context, no one could preach any better.[12]

The importance of context was driven home to me just recently. A few months ago I moved to a new church. During the first few months I used several old sermons in order to get acquainted with my new turf. I discovered, however, that in most cases the old sermons had to be revised. The new context demanded changes in the sermons.

Being relevant in a local setting means we need to be tuned in to the needs of the hour. An old Jewish story tells about a conversation between two different groups of rabbinic disciples. One group boasted that they stayed awake all night between Thursday and Friday, that on Friday they gave alms in proportion to what they had, and that on the sabbath they recited the entire Book of Psalms.

A disciple from the other group replied: "We stay awake every night as long as we can; we give alms whenever we run across a poor man and happen to have money in our pockets; and we do not say the psalms it took David seventy years of hard work to make, all in a row, but according to the needs of the hour."[13]

A good pastor will preach sermons "according to the needs of the hour." To do this he must know his people and his community and attempt to bring an appropriate word from Holy Scripture.

Several years ago numerous members of my congregation were suffering serious illnesses. I felt the need to address their plight in my preaching. I developed a sermon series called "Illness Through the Eyes of Faith."[14]

Another time found our community in economic crisis. We were anxious. The future was uncertain. My preaching took me to Abraham's struggle of faith as he faced an unknown future.

The first sermon, "Faith Is Born," dealt with Abraham's initial call to faith and his response. My texts were Hebrews 11:1-2,8-10 and Genesis 12:1-4.

The second sermon, "Faith in Struggle" acknowledged that faith often struggles in the face of difficulty. I introduced the sermon this way:

Faith was born in my life at age 16. My old Buick convertible expressed my newfound faith. On the front license plate a sign said, "God Is Alive." On the back, a bumper sticker said, "Christ is the answer." Next to the radio was a picture of a fishhook. The caption read, "I'm hooked on Jesus." And on the glove box was a magnet which said, "God said it, I believe it, that settles it!" Faith was so simple then, and I was so sure.

That was a long time ago. I still have faith—faith much deeper than bumper sticker theology. But life and faith aren't so simple anymore. The world is more complex. I've asked some hard questions, learned about life's limitations, preached a lot of funerals, prayed with too many cancer patients, and had some dreams die.

I spoke openly about the struggles our community was facing and how it was also a faith struggle. I then turned to the text, Genesis 12:10 and 17:15-19, and spoke about Abraham's struggle with faith. The theme of the sermon could be summarized, "I believe; help my unbelief."

The third and final sermon, "Faith Matured," finds Abraham's faith tested and proved. The text was Genesis 22:1-18, the story of Abraham's journey to Mount Moriah to sacrifice his son Isaac. The central theme of the sermon was that mature faith believes that God will provide grace for the journey regardless of how painful that journey may be. After an opening illustration and a few comments to set the stage, I continued:

And so the journey began up the "wild and windy" mountain, up the mountain of God forsakenness. Abraham's emotions churning, his faith in absolute anguish, he climbed on. Isaac said to his daddy, "Behold, the fire and the wood, but where is the lamb for a burnt offering?" (v. 7)

How did Abraham stand it? How could anybody? All of us, however, have to walk up Mount Moriah at some time in our lives. Times come when we, like Abraham, are anguished and in despair; times when darkness engulfs us and God seems far away; times when we walk up the mountains of death and grief, broken dreams, terminal illnesses, broken relationships, failures, depression, and feelings of hopelessness. If you haven't yet walked up Mount Moriah, you will.

"Daddy, where is the lamb for the offering?" The words cut into Abraham's heart like a thrusting knife. His faith was in anguish.

How do we have faith at such times? What do we do in

the face of the absurdities and contradictions of life? God had promised to give a son. Now the promise, the hope, the dream was dying. How do we survive when we climb our Mount Moriahs of God forsakenness and despair?

The answer for Abraham was faith. On that mountain Abraham's faith reached its peak, its highest level of maturity. "Daddy, where is the lamb for the burnt offering?" Abraham said, "God will provide."

Faith at its most mature level is believing that God will provide. Abraham didn't know how God would do it; he just believed he would. Somehow. Some way. He didn't know how, but he trusted. And trust is the essence of faith.

So Abraham built an altar. And then he did the seemingly impossible; he laid his beloved son on the altar, took the knife, and prepared to do the unthinkable. Somehow in that dark hour he trusted God.

And God did provide. Just as Abraham was preparing to thrust the knife downward, God called out: " 'Abraham, Abraham! Do not lay your hand on the lad.' And Abraham lifted up his eyes and looked, and behold, behind him was a ram, caught in a thicket by his horns; and Abraham went and took the ram, and offered it up as a burnt offering instead of his son" (vv. 12-13).

God provided. "So Abraham called the name of that place The Lord will provide" (v. 14).

Abraham would face at least two more Mount Moriahs in his life, one at the death of his wife Sarah and again at his own death. And Abraham would learn that God does provide even when we face "the valley of the shadow of death."

So the story ends where it began. Abraham trusted God for the unknown. He believed God would provide whatever was needed for the journey.

God does provide. I've heard that testimony many times.

From a pastor whose two sons drowned in a frozen pond one dark January day. That was his Mount Moriah. And he learned that God provides. God gave him the strength to walk through the grief and pain and anger.

From Grady Nutt's wife after Grady died in a plane crash. God's provision was friends who helped her make it through the anguish of her Mount Moriah.

From the widows of our church who discovered God's provision when their husbands died. God gave them the strength to "walk and not faint" through the love and prayers of their church.

From terminally ill cancer patients, who, even in their pain and struggle, experienced the presence of God.

From the man who wept at the collapse of his business yet found God's grace sufficient to carry him through.

From divorced persons who, in spite of their pain and fear, discovered that God could give them a new future.

And that same God will also provide us with sufficient grace to survive these turbulent and uncertain days in our community.

Abraham believed that God would provide. His faith had matured. Although this insight came late in his life, others learn it at a young age.

A little black girl was scheduled to have her tonsils removed. She was rolled into the operating room and placed on the table. The doctor started to put her to sleep. She asked, "Can I sing first?"

"Of course," said the doctor.

She sang, "He's got the whole world in His hands, He's got the whole world in His hands, He's got the whole world in His hands, He's got the whole world in His hands." She then sang, "He's got you and me sister in His hands, He's got you and me sister in His hands, He's got you and me sister in His hands, He's got the whole world in His hands." The doctor proceeded to put her to sleep.

"I'm not finished yet," she said.

Then she sang, "He's got the tiny little baby in His hands, He's got the tiny little baby in His hands, He's got the tiny little baby in His hands, He's got the whole world in His hands."

"OK," she said, "I'm ready." (Note: I actually sang the verses of this song and asked the congregation to join me. It proved to be a moving conclusion to the sermon).

These are just a few examples, but they help illustrate the principle of relevance—both universal and local. When I think about this principle I recall a story Vernon Davis, dean of Midwestern Baptist Theological Seminary, tells from his days in the pastorate.

Dr. Davis had just arrived at a new church. He went to visit one of the oldest and most faithful members. She told him: "Brother Davis, when you preach to us on Sunday morning, we'll all be wearing nice clothes and a big smile. But don't let that fool you. Just remember that under every heart is a little pail of tears."

If we'll speak to the "little pail of tears," as well as to the joys and other significant issues of life, our preaching will be relevant and meaningful.

Notes

1. Henri J. M. Nouwen, *The Wounded Healer* (Garden City, New York: Image Books, 1979), 39.

2. Henry Grady Davis, *Design for Preaching* (Philadelphia: Muhlenberg Press, 1958), 43.

3. Frederick Buechner, *Telling the Truth: the Gospel as Tragedy, Comedy and Fairy Tale* (New York: Harper and Row, 1977), 23.

4. Edgar Jackson, *How to Preach to People's Needs* (Nashville: Abingdon Press, 1956), 23.

5. Harold Kushner, *When All You've Ever Wanted Isn't Enough: the Search for a Life that Matters* (New York: Pocket Books, 1986).

6. Ibid, 43.

7. Ibid, 144-45.

8. Robert J. Hastings, *Tinyburg Tales* (Nashville: Broadman Press, 1983), 66.

9. Kushner, 158.

10. Martin E. Marty, quoting from Criterion in *Context*, Clarion Publications, August 1 and 15, 1981.

11. Fred B. Craddock, *As One Without Authority* (Nashville: Abingdon, 1983).

12. *Leadership*, Summer 1987, vol. 8, no. 3, 19.

13. Martin Buber, *Tales of the Hasidim: the Later Masters* (New York: Schocken Books, 1948), 285-286.

14. *Proclaim*, Oct. Nov. Dec., 1988, vol. 19, no. 1, 20-25.

3 ENGAGING PREACH

A friend recently wrote, "I went to church last Sunday and wasn't bored." This was a newsworthy report because my friend associates church attendance and sermons with unbearable boredom. So do lots of other folks. As Fred Craddock points out, however, "What is true does not always have to bore one to death."[1]

If we want people to listen to our sermons, they must be interesting. Good preaching should be planned and relevant. It must also be engaging. The secret to engaging sermons is using stories and illustrations. That's not the only factor, of course. Interesting sermons also have solid content, good movement, and are well delivered. But illustrations are a primary ingredient in engaging sermons and will be the focus of this chapter.

Using stories and illustrations in preaching follows biblical precedent. One reason the Bible is so powerful is its rich imagery. Short stories and parables were Jesus' primary mode of teaching. Someone once figured that the Gospel of Luke is 52 percent parables. If Jesus relied so heavily on illustrative material, surely we should do the same.

Illustrations are an important element of every sermon. Their purpose is not entertainment but effective communication of God's message. Illustrations spark interest, hold attention, clarify meaning, relate biblical truth to real life, touch emotions, give needed breaks and rests to the congregation, drive home the point and make the sermon memorable. Illustrations help make the introduction, conclusion, and body of a sermon more engaging.

The Introduction

An old recipe for rabbit pie begins with the instruction to "first catch a rabbit." Similarly, the would-be preacher must "first catch the attention of the audience."[2] A good illustration does exactly that. Humorous illustrations are especially effective. They help break the ice, gain interest, and introduce the subject.

A few weeks ago, I heard the following story. It's an old illustration, but it was new to me. I plan to use it the next time I preach about grace and mercy.

A woman went to a photographer to have her picture taken. Although she considered herself attractive, she was actually rather plain.

As she posed for the picture, she told the photographer, "Young man, make sure to do me justice."

"Madam," he replied, "you don't need justice; you need mercy!"

I began a sermon on the subject of adolescence with a quote from James Dobson. He described adolescence as "a time of indigestion, heartburn and trauma," which "offers something painful for everybody."[3]

We recently observed Senior Adult Day in my church. I began my sermon with a story about the famous writer Agatha Christie. When asked what she thought about being married to Lord Mallowan, an archaeologist, she replied: "It's wonderful. The older I get, the more interested he is in me."[4]

I told the following story when I began a sermon on pride and status.

> CBS made Gary Moore a vice-president of their network in recognition for his many years of service on television. One of his friends told him that wasn't such a big deal, that TV networks hand out titles like they do gold watches. Moore didn't believe him. His friend worked for the National Biscuit Company and said, "Our company has a vice-president in charge of Fig Newtons." Moore didn't believe it. His friend said, "Call over there and ask for him."
>
> Moore took the phone and called the National Biscuit Company. He said, "I'd like to speak to the vice-president in charge of Fig Newtons." He was shocked when the receptionist said, "Is that packaged Fig Newtons or bulk Fig Newtons?"[5]

Death is a difficult subject. Perhaps that's why we make so many jokes about it. A humorous story about this serious subject can be an effective way to begin a sermon on death.

A certain woman married a wealthy man. After he died, she received his entire estate. She then married an actor. They had many happy years together, going to Broadway shows and other theatrical events. After he died, she married a minister. She became interested in spiritual matters while married to this minister; but he, like the others, also died. Finally she married a funeral director. After several years of marriage, she died and he buried her.

When an acquaintance of this woman reflected on her four husbands—a millionaire, an actor, a minister, and a funeral director, he said, "She married one for the money, two for the show, three to get ready, and four to go!"

I used the following story for a sermon on the third

chapter of James concerning the tongue. A woman stopped her pastor after church. She was a notorious gossip. She said: "Pastor, the Lord has convicted me of my sin of gossip. My tongue is getting me and others in trouble."

Her pastor knew she was not sincere because she had gone through that routine many times before. He asked, "Well, what are you going to do about it?"

'I want to give my tongue to God," she said. "I want to lay my tongue on the altar.

Her pastor replied, "There isn't an altar big enough."

Humor is an excellent way to begin sermons on marriage and family. A certain husband determined to show real love for his wife because he hadn't been a loving husband lately. He came home early with flowers and candy, rang the doorbell, and, when his wife opened the door he sang, "I love you truly." His wife said: "Oh Harold, this has been a rotten day. The phone has rung off the wall, the roast has burned, the kids have been awful, and now you come home drunk!"[6]

An illustration on prayer comes from an old rabbinic story. A man told a rabbi about his poverty and troubles. "Don't worry," advised the rabbi. "Pray to God with all your heart, and the merciful Lord will have mercy upon you."

"But I don't know how to pray," said the man.

"Then," the rabbi said, "you have a great deal to worry about."[7]

I began a sermon on the dangers of being too busy by telling the following story. A man who was a top executive with a telegraph company went on a trip. It was extremely cold outside when he arrived at the bus station, so he went into a local telegraph station hoping to get warmed up. When he got inside, however, it was cold.

He noticed that there was no fire in the fireplace. He said to the young telegraph operator, "Why don't you build a fire in this place and warm it up?"

The young man said, "Listen mister, I'm too busy sending telegrams to build fires."

The man then told this boy that he was the vice-president of the company and that he wanted him to send a telegram to the home office at once. The message was, "Fire this man immediately."

A moment later the young telegraph operator brought a load of wood into the office and began to build a fire. The executive asked, "Young man, have you sent that telegram yet?"

The young telegraph operator said, "Listen mister, I'm too busy building fires to send telegrams."

Resigning from my church a few months ago was a difficult and emotional time. To ease myself and the entire congregation, I began with this story.

The new preacher had just arrived. As he moved into his office, he discovered three envelopes and a letter in his drawer. They were from the previous pastor. The letter said, "When it gets bad, open envelope number one. When it gets really bad, open envelope number two. When it becomes unbearable, open envelope number three."

At first, the preacher didn't think much about the note and the three envelopes. After a year, however, things got bad. He remembered the note and opened envelope number one. It said, "Blame the previous pastor." He did, and it worked. About a year later, however, things got really bad. He opened envelope number two. It said, 'Blame the denomination." He did, and it worked once again. But after three years things became unbearable. He hated to use up the last envelope but had no choice.

The message of the third envelope was, "Prepare three envelopes."

After a good laugh, both my congregation and I were better prepared for the hard task of resigning. I went back to visit my previous church a few weeks ago, and one of the members asked if I had discovered three envelopes at my new church!

Of course, opening illustrations don't have to be humorous. Sometimes humor would be out of place. Last year I preached the sermon for our community-wide Good Friday service. When I came to the pulpit, several passion narratives from the Gospels had recently been read and we had just sung, "When I Survey the Wondrous Cross." It was no time for humor. I began the sermon with a serious illustration which is found later in this book.

Several years ago my church wrote a statement of purpose. We decided to highlight it in our worship services. I preached for five Sundays on the mission of our church. I began the series with the following illustration.

Several years ago I had a long discussion with a Vietnam veteran. He said: "When I first went to Vietnam, I had a clear sense of purpose. I was going to save the world from communism. When I got there, however, and saw the insanity of the war, my sense of purpose was destroyed. After awhile I developed a new purpose, to survive another day."

"If we're not careful," I said, "we can have a similar experience in our church. We can lose sight of our purpose and develop a survival and status-quo mentality. So over the next five weeks, let's focus again on the mission of our church."

I mentioned in a previous chapter about the death of a teenager in my church. His funeral was on a Friday. I had planned to preach a stewardship sermon that Sunday.

Obviously, that was not appropriate. I changed my sermon that Sunday to "The Just Still Live by Faith." I began the sermon by saying, "I didn't plan on preaching this sermon today. But on Friday we buried Anthony. I've never preached a funeral for an 18-year-old before. I hope I never have to again." By speaking about the subject that was on everybody's mind, I was able to bring a relevant sermon to my congregation. It proved to be one of the most moving worship services our church ever had.

I began a Father's Day sermon once by telling about a YMCA in Louisville, Kentucky. Above the front door is a sign which says, "What does it profit to gain the whole world, but lose your own son."

The sermon for Memorial Day weekend was on grief. I began by telling about Pearl Buck's novel *The Mother*. In this story a son leads his mother to a cemetery. She is mourning the loss of her youngest son. She tells her older son, "Go away and leave me for awhile and let me weep." The elder son hesitates, but the mother insists, "Leave me, for if I do not weep, then I must die."[8] The stage was now set for a sermon on the pain of grief and some of the resources available to face it.

I began a series of sermons of the great doctrines of the Christian faith by citing an educational film which had just aired on public television. It was a documentary on the Jewish nation called "Civilization and the Jews." The show discussed the turbulent history of Israel. Their history is a story of struggle. Early in their nation's history their homeland was captured, their people deported and scattered all over the world. In spite of the fact that they had no place to call home, the Jewish people survived and retained their identity. The great empires rose and fell, but these scattered people stood. How did this happen? What was it that kept them together? The television show pointed out that it was their belief system which held them together—their belief in one sovereign God and in the law of God with its ethical and ritual demands. With that I began my series on the central doctrines of our faith.

One week after Easter, I preached a sermon on Thomas and his struggle with doubt. I began by quoting Martin Luther, "He who doesn't think he believes, but is in despair, has the greatest faith."[9]

One particular Sunday found my community in despair. Another major business was closing down, and folks were extremely anxious and depressed. The truth is, none of us felt like worshiping. My sermon was on worshiping God even when we don't feel like it. I began with a rabbinic story. An old rabbi had been weeping. He cried, "Father, Father, lead us from our exile . . ." All wept with him. But after a while, he roused himself and cried, "Now let us delight our Father and show him that his children can dance, even though they are in darkness." He gave orders to play a merry tune and began to dance.[10]

I said, "How can we dance today given our worries and problems?" I continued with a second illustration similar to the first. Soon after the death of a rabbi's wife, his daughter also died. In the midst of his grief he prayed: "Lord of the world, you took my wife from me. But I still had my daughter and could rejoice in her. Now you have taken her from me, too. Now I have no one left to rejoice in, except you alone. So I shall rejoice in you."[11]

These are just a few examples of how illustrations can be an effective introduction to your sermon. They are equally important during the body and conclusion.

The Body

The longer I preach, the less interested I am in sermon points. What I'm mostly concerned with is making one point—one major thrust. Yet having several points is still a valid way to preach and I do it often. When making several points, however, one needs to support an overall point or theme. And illustrations are a helpful way to do it.

My recent sermon on the Fourth Commandment helps to demonstrate how illustrations can build the body of a sermon. This sermon was part of a series on the Ten Commandments. This was my least favorite of the series. I don't hold it up as a model. But it demonstrates how illustrations can help even an average sermon become more engaging and thus more effective. The basic point of the sermon was the importance of observing the sabbath. The title of the sermon was "A Special Day." I noted that the sabbath was a day to rest, relate, and remember. Although it was a workable outline, it wasn't very exciting. I tried to spruce it up a bit by starting with the following story.

A young boy enjoyed going to his grandparents' house on Sunday afternoons. After church all his aunts, uncles, cousins, and grandparents would gather at his grandfather's house. They ate a huge, delicious meal and spent the rest of the day playing.

But not the women. They worked all day in the kitchen. This didn't seem fair to the boy. One Sunday afternoon, while the women worked in the kitchen, he asked his grandfather about this. "Granddad, the women sure work hard on Sunday. Doesn't the Bible say we shouldn't work on Sundays?"

His grandfather smiled and said, "Bring that Bible to

me." The boy brought the family Bible to his grandfather, and the old man opened it up to our text for today, Exodus 20:8-11. "Now look real close," he said. "In verse 10, it says you shall not do any work (and that's talking about us) nor your son, nor your daughter, nor your servants, nor your cattle, nor the sojourner. But it doesn't say a thing about your wife or your mother. So, you see, it's OK for the women to work on Sunday!"

After a few other introductory remarks, I moved into the body of the sermon. Under point one, the sabbath as a day to rest, I used the following illustration. It came from a film about a man who designed aircraft.

In this scene a pilot was performing amazing feats for the people watching below. He was doing double and triple loops and other tricks. But when he landed, he broke a strut on his plane. He jumped in another plane and gunned the motor. The designer, seeing him do this, shouted and waved for him to stop. The pilot, adrenaline flowing, ignored him and roared off into the sky. The designer said, "That plane will never stand it." And true enough, as the pilot was doing a sharp loop, a wing broke off and the plane crashed. Someone standing near the designer asked, "How did you know?"

"I built that plane," came the reply.[12]

I reminded the congregation that God designed and built the human body and that He knew we could not take constant stress. Thus, He gave us the sabbath as a day of rest.

The second point was that the sabbath was a day to relate. As Leviticus 23:3 says, the sabbath is a "holy convocation." In the Book of Hebrews we are told not to forsake "the assembling of ourselves together"(10:25, KJV). Numerous illustrations could be used for this point. I simply found a canned one from a preaching magazine.

> A famous organist was asked to give several concerts using an old-fashioned pump organ. The bellows of the organ had to be pumped by hand, so the organist hired a boy to stand behind the organ and pump while he played. After the first concert, the boy said to the organist, "We sure played good tonight."
>
> "What do you mean, 'we'? I was the one who played, not you!"
>
> At the next concert, the organist sat down and began to play, but no sound came. He kept pressing down on the keys but nothing happened. It finally dawned on him that there was no air in the bellows. The organist whispered to the boy behind the organ, "Pump."
>
> The boy responded in a whispered tone, "Say we."[13]

I reminded the congregation that the sabbath forces us to "say we." It reminds us that none of us are self-sufficient and that we need one another desperately.

The final point was that the sabbath is a day to remember God and worship Him. I told about a church which had a parking problem. It was rapidly outgrowing its limited parking space. Nearby was a large supermarket that had ample parking space which was not used on Sunday. The church secured permission to use the grocery story parking lot on Sundays. The owner of the store, however, wanted a written agreement. He added one stipulation. The contract said that the church could use the parking lot on only 51 Sundays a year. One Sunday out of the year had to be designated a "no-parking Sunday." He said: "For 51 Sundays, I make no charge. I give it to you free. But one day a year I want you to remember who gave it to you."[14] The sabbath, I remarked, is a time to remember God who gave us life, offer our thanks, and worship Him.

This was the weakest sermon of the series, and these were not exceptional illustrations. But by the use of these illustrations, I was able to make the sermon more engaging and better communicated the importance of observing the sabbath.

Let me offer another example. For Advent last year I preached a series of sermons on the characters of the nativity. I called the series "The Manger People." The title of the series came from a story by Wayne Price. One Christmas his children received a set of tiny nativity figures. They kept the figures in a cigar box. Periodically, throughout the year, one of them would get the box from the shelf and say, "Daddy, tell us the story about the manger people."[15]

One of the sermons focused on Mary and Joseph. The sermon revolved around two themes—Christmas as a problem and Christmas as a promise. The illustrations primarily came from the text, Matthew 1:18 to 2:23.

The first Christmas was full of struggle, pain, and trauma. In our romanticism of the season, we sometimes lose sight of the many negatives Mary, Joseph, and others experienced.

I began the sermon by mentioning the well-known Charlie Brown Christmas program. In their annual television special, Charlie Brown just can't get into the Christmas spirit. Thus Linus observes, "Charlie Brown, you're the only person I know who can take a wonderful season like Christmas and turn it into a problem."

Christmas, however, is a problem for many folks, just as it was for Mary and Joseph. I developed that theme with the text and contemporary examples in our community.

In the midst of all the problems and tragedy of the first Christmas, however, was also a promise. Mary and Joseph were given a promise: "For that which is conceived in her is of the Holy Spirit, she will bear a son, and you shall call his name Jesus, for he will save his people from their sins. . . . and his name shall be called Emmanuel (which means, God with us)"(vv. 21- 23).

Christmas promises God's presence whatever the circumstances. Regardless of what problems we may face, God is with us. To help illustrate this point, I used a familiar Christmas story concerning George Frederick Handel.

Most people have heard of this great musician. Late in life things turned sour for Handel. The great composer lost his fortune, his health, and nearly all hope. Critics claimed that Handel was burned-out, old, and outdated—a has-been. He was threatened with debtors' prison and was about out of hope.

About that time Charles Jennens, a wealthy friend and writer, asked Handel to compose music and orchestration for a musical score on the biblical theme of redemption. The text was completely Scripture. And Handel, old and worn as he was, mustered enough grace to write the epic, *Messiah*. He thought it would take a year to write, but he became inspired. He worked day and night and completed the project, all 260 pages of manuscript, in only twenty-four days. He fought back from failure to make his greatest contribution to the world's music. To one without a song, God's good news of redemption gave Handel the inspiration to write *Messiah*.[16]

The Conclusion

Illustrations can also add interest and strength to a sermon's conclusion. I usually try to end my sermons with an illustration which pulls together the major ideas. Several examples follow.

I mentioned earlier my sermon on the Fourth Commandment. This is the way I concluded the sermon.

A long time ago, when the broadcasting industry was still in its infancy, a letter was sent to the National Broadcasting Company from a prospector in the hills of Montana. Written on a piece of brown bag that had been folded into an envelope, it contained an unusual request. "I am a regular listener to your programs; and as a friend, I want to ask you for a favor. It gets lonely up here and besides my radio and my dog I have not much else for company. I do have a violin that I used to play, but now it is badly out of tune. Would you please be kind enough at seven o'clock next Sunday night to strike me an A so I can put that fiddle back into tune?" The following Sunday night, at seven o'clock sharp, the network interrupted its scheduled programming to sound an "A" and give a friend his pitch.[17]

I reminded my congregation that God gave us the sabbath to keep our lives in tune—in tune physically as we rest, in tune relationally as we relate with the Christian community, and in tune spiritually as we remember God and worship Him.

I once concluded a sermon on the Christian family with an illustration from the Civil War. This story was told by former President Jimmy Carter at an annual meeting of the Christian Life Commission of the Southern Baptist Convention. That year's theme was the family.

In one of the crucial battles in the war between the states, the two sides lined up one night, waiting for the next day's battle. During the night the bands had a "battle of the bands." The Union band first played "Rally 'Round the Flag, Boys," and after a moment of silence the

Confederate band played "The Bonny Blue Flag." Then the Union band played "Hail Columbia," and the Confederates came back with "Maryland, My Maryland." Then the Yankees played "The Star-Spangled Banner," and the rebels replied with what else but "Dixie." Finally, the Union band started playing "Home, Sweet Home," and after a few minutes they realized the Confederates were playing along with them. No matter what their differences may be, people hold home dear to their hearts.

John Killinger, pastor of the First Congregational Church of Los Angeles, is a master at these kinds of closing illustrations. I received a sermon in the mail from him just this morning. His subject was the church. He concluded his sermon this way.

An old physician who had gone as a missionary doctor to the hills of Eastern Kentucky in the days of the depression told me about a new church building he had seen erected there. It was a simple, white-clapboard church with a single, all-purpose room. A small choir loft in the chancel doubled as a Sunday School room. Before the choir loft was a simple platform; and at the front center of the platform stood the pulpit, constructed of white oak. Three chairs were on the platform, one large one in the center and two smaller ones on the sides. The minister sat in one of the chairs on the side, and the song leader sat in the other. Someone wanted to know why they had the big chair in the middle, because no one ever sat in it. That, explained the preacher, was "the Jesus chair." It was put there to remind the congregation whenever they gathered that the Lord was the unseen Guest at every meeting, at every worship service, in every situation.

The Jesus chair. Maybe every church ought to have one. Then we wouldn't worry about Robert's *Rules of*

Order because we would remember Jesus' Rules of Order. Then we would be less like the disciples in the upper room and more like all those folks at Pentecost. The Jesus chair would remind us of the cross and the resurrection—and they make all the difference in the world![18]

The above examples demonstrate how illustrations can be effectively used in the introduction, body, and conclusion of your sermons. They help demonstrate the value of illustrations in communicating the gospel.

Where to Find Illustrations

Most preachers understand the importance of illustrations in preaching. The problem is finding them. Where can a preacher find illustrations? Everywhere! I find mine from at least nine different sources.

The Bible

This is so obvious it hardly needs to be mentioned. But Holy Scripture is one of the best resources available for finding illustrations. One of the great advantages of biblical illustrations is their authority. You can use isolated illustrations to support your points or allow the entire text to be an ongoing illustration, such as the parable of the prodigal son. One of my favorite illustration resources is *Nave's Topical Bible*.[19] Hundreds of different subjects are listed. Following the subject heading are numerous Scripture passages on that subject. *Nave's Topical Bible* ought to be in every pastor's study.

Personal Experiences

Personal experiences offer an excellent resource for illustrations. Preachers ought constantly to be on the lookout for them while they go about their daily lives.

Illustrations abound for the preacher with eyes to see and ears to hear.

Last year, while waiting in line at the post office, the woman in front of me asked the postal clerk for some secular Christmas stamps.

"What?" he asked.

"I'd like some some secular Christmas stamps," she replied. He still looked puzzled.

"Secular," she said, "not sacred." Advent began that Sunday, and I now had my opening illustration.

A few months ago my three-year-old daughter, Laura, and I watched a sunset. She said, "God is putting the sun to bed."

"That's right," I responded.

"Daddies cannot do that," she said.

A few weeks later, when I preached on the glory of God, I used that incident as an illustration.

While preparing a sermon on the grace and forgiveness of God, I recalled a childhood experience which taught me much about the subject. It proved to be an effective illustration.

Influenced by peer pressure, I had been stealing from a local dime store for several weeks. No grand larceny, mind you, but stealing all the same. I stole a candy bar one day, an inexpensive toy the next, and so on. On this particular day I stole a plastic ring. It cost less than a dime, and I had a dollar in my pocket; but an eight-year-old boy will do foolish things to impress his friends and to feel he belongs to the group.

The moment I slipped the ring into my pocket, the store manager abruptly grabbed me and demanded my name and phone number. My mother arrived shortly, embarrassed and livid with anger. I felt ashamed. It was one of the most traumatic experiences of my brief eight years.

The drive home was unbearably long. The first item on the agenda was the hairbrush. Spankings by the hairbrush were reserved only for the most serious infractions. After the spanking I was sent to my room.

As I sat in my room crying, I felt an awesome sense of guilt. For the first time in my life I doubted my mother's love for me. I felt I had done something so awful, so terrible, that she would no longer love me. I picked up a pencil and a Big Chief writing pad and wrote my mother a note saying: "Mommy, I'm sorry. Do you still love me?"

Transporting the message, however, was a problem. I was upstairs, and Mom was downstairs. Finally, I came up with an ingenious plan. I folded the note into a paper airplane, opened my door, and sailed the message of repentance down the stairs. I sat on my bed and continued to feel deep remorse for my actions.

Soon my mother came into my room. She had been crying. She walked to my bed, looked at me, and began to weep. Then she took me in her arms and said: "Yes, Honey, I still love you. I love you more than anything in the world."

As we embraced, I felt a sense of love and forgiveness I will never forget. That experience is burned into my memory and will vividly live there the rest of my life. Telling this story evoked the interest and emotions of my congregation and helped communicate the unconditional love of God that my sermon addressed.

While we should not overdo personal experiences, if done occasionally and in good taste, they are perfectly appropriate. When you use personal illustrations, make sure they happened to you and not to somebody else. It lacks integrity to say something happened to us when it actually happened to somebody else. It does not hurt the illustration to say it happened to someone else and in so doing you preserve your integrity. Obviously you'll want to use illustrations which are appropriate and which didn't embarrass anybody or break confidence.

Movies

Movies are one of my favorite sources for finding illustrations. Just last night I watched an old rerun of *All That Jazz*. This somewhat bizarre movie about life on Broadway was actually about death. The main character was a Broadway choreographer. Although tremendously successful in his career, his personal life was in shambles—relationally and physically. Finally, the endless drinking, smoking, drugs, and affairs caught up with him. He had a heart attack and was dying.

Near the end of the movie, he speaks to a hospital aide about his life. He says: "It's just a rough cut. I need more time." He, like so many others, get to the end of life and realize how much was left undone and done wrong. He saw the "rough cut" and wanted more time to revise and edit; but it was too late. The only way to avoid such an ending is to do what's important today, while there is still time.

Years ago, a movie was released called *The Elephant Man*. It was based on the true and remarkable story of John Merrick. Through a tragic birth defect, John Merrick was a grotesque figure. His head and face were horribly deformed, his skin all boiled over, his spine curved in a hideous fashion. For years he was a freak in a carnival show.

Through a series of events, a doctor became interested in the Elephant Man. We learn that this "freak" is a sensitive, intelligent, and loving person. The hospital becomes his home. During his stay at the hospital a lovely woman actress becomes his friend. One day she brought John a book of Shakespeare's plays. Moved by the gift, he immediately opened the book and began to read from the classic play, *Romeo and Juliet.* The woman, being an actress, knew the lines by heart. John read the lines of Romeo, and she responded with the lines of Juliet. When it came to the part where Romeo and Juliet kissed, this woman, in great love, care, and acceptance, kissed the Elephant Man in spite of his terrible ugliness.

She said to him, "John, you're not the Elephant Man." He replied, "I'm not?"

"No," she said, "you are Romeo!"

This story served as a beautiful parable of grace and was well received by the congregation.

The old classic *Cat on a Hot Tin Roof* can serve as a powerful illustration on the true meaning of success. Success has little to do with wealth and power and much to do with relationships and meaning.

The movie is about an old man and his family. The man was rich and powerful; everyone called him Big Daddy. He had all the things money could buy. He also had cancer of the colon and an alcoholic son.

The end of the movie finds Big Daddy and his son in the basement of his mansion. For one brief moment Big Daddy's masks of power, wealth, and success are stripped away. We realize he's not successful at all. His relationship with his wife was shallow; he was estranged from his son; and his daughter's only concern was getting the lion's share of Big Daddy's estate. He had no significant relationships. He didn't even know the names of his servants. He knew no love, no purpose in life, no meaning. What did he have? A basement full of expensive antiques.

A few weeks ago I preached a sermon on our need to adapt and adjust to life's changes and problems. I used the old movie *The Monty Stratton Story* as an illustration.

The movie tells the story of Monty Stratton, a pitcher for the Chicago White Sox in the old American League. Monty was an extremely successful baseball player. He also had a happy marriage. Life was going well for Monty. But then, as it does so often, tragedy struck. Monty went on a hunting trip and accidently shot himself in the leg. In order to save his life, the doctors finally had to amputate his leg.

Monty was crushed. He became depressed and felt that life was over. But then he decided he could adjust. "They took my leg," he said to himself, "not my arm. I can still pitch." So he got an artificial leg and began to learn how to pitch again.

Learning to pitch with an artificial leg was difficult. He practiced endless hours. At first, his wife caught for him. His pitches were so hard, however, that he knocked her to the ground whenever she caught the ball. She finally had to quit. Monty said, "I've never had a catcher quit on me before."

"Yes," she said, "but you've never had a catcher before who was three months pregnant!"

In order to practice his pitching, Monty hung an old wash basin on the side of his barn and threw pitches into it. He got his old dog to fetch the balls for him.

Day after day, week after week, Monty adjusted and adapted to the loss of his leg and learned to pitch again. Finally, he was able to play in a real game. His pitching was fine, but he had a hard time batting. He got a hit but fell to the ground as he tried to run to first base. The crowd sat in silence. When he returned to the dugout, the players didn't know how to react. Monty finally broke the ice and said, "I guess I started my slide too soon!"

Monty didn't let the loss of his leg ruin his life. He adjusted and went on with living. At the end of the movie Monty's team was playing a big game. At the bottom of the ninth inning, they were down by one run. They had two outs, and the bases were loaded. It was Monty's turn to bat. The coach started to send in a pinch hitter, but the team said, "No, let Monty bat." As he walked to the mound, team members said to Monty, "Go get us one." Monty walked to the plate, got a hit, and knocked in two men to win the game.

These examples demonstrate how movies can be sources of effective illustrations. Next time you watch "Saturday Night at the Movies," remember that it might help you get ready for Sunday's sermon!

Television

Occasionally, a good illustration can be found while watching TV. Such was the case of the following "Family Ties" show.

In this episode, Alex's friend is killed in a car accident. The entire show is Alex's struggle with death—his friend's and his own. At one point he cries out: "I don't want to die! I don't just mean that I don't want to die young. I don't want to die middle-aged. I don't want to die old. I don't want to die!"

Early in the show a man (who the audience never sees) asks Alex, "Do you believe in God?"

At first, Alex says, "I don't want to talk about that."

But at the end of the show, the unseen man asks again, "Alex, do you believe in God?"

Finally, Alex says: "That's the issue, isn't it? That's the bottom line of the whole deal."

A few months ago my 10-year-old son and I watched an episode of the popular TV comedy "Alf". In this episode, Alf (a cute alien who is also a TV addict) fantasizes living on Gilligan's Island. Life on Gilligan's Island, he tells himself, is exciting, invigorating, and thrilling. Life where he is—the Tanner family—is boring, predictable, and an overall drag. Finally, Alf gets his wish. He ends up on Gilligan's Island only to discover that life there isn't what he expected. Indeed, the folks on Gilligan's Island, tired and bored with life on a marooned island, fantasize living at the Tanner home!

I laughed because the show was so true to life. So often we think life is happening somewhere we are not. We work hard to get there only to discover when we arrive that it isn't so great there after all. Happiness remains elusive.

I used this illustration when I preached on Jeremiah's letter to the exiles. The point of the sermon was that if we're going to live, we better do it in the here and now, because that's all we have. The exiles could only think about the future. *When we get back home*, they thought, *then we'll really live.* But what a tragedy to waste all those years in exile. They could have had a good life where they were. And as we know, even when they did go home, it wasn't as great as they had hoped. So Jeremiah gave them this message from God: "Build houses and live in them; plant gardens and eat their produce. Take wives and have sons and daughters . . . multiply there, and do not decrease. But seek the welfare of the city where I have sent you into exile, and pray to the Lord on its behalf, for in its welfare you will find your welfare" (Jer. 29:5-7).

Books

Reading   provides   a   tremendous   resource   for

illustrations. My illustration file is packed with illustrations which I discovered in various books. Take nonfiction books for example. Many are full of illustrative material. I mentioned earlier Harold Kushner's book *When All You've Ever Wanted Isn't Enough.* Some of the best illustrations I've discovered in a long time were in that book. Three have already been mentioned. Let me share two more.

Kushner tells about sitting on a beach one summer day and watching two children, a boy and a girl, playing in the sand. They were hard at work building an elaborate sand castle by the water's edge, with gates and towers and moats and internal passages. Just when they had nearly finished their project, a big wave came along and knocked it down, reducing it to a heap of wet sand. He expected the children to burst into tears, devastated by what had happened to all their hard work. But they surprised him. Instead, they held each other's hands, laughed, and sat down to build another castle.

Kushner learned an important lesson from those children. All the things in our lives, all the complicated structures we spend so much time and energy creating, are built on sand. Only our relationships to other people endure. Sooner or later, a wave will come along and knock down what we have worked so hard to build. When that happens, only the person who has somebody's hand to hold will be able to laugh.[20]

Another story in this book tells about a young man who ran away from his conventional middle-class home to join the Unification Church. When asked why he did it, he said: "My father only talks about getting into college and getting a good job. Reverend Moon talks to me about helping him save the world."[21]

Another nonfiction book full of possible illustrations is

William Barclay's *A Spiritual Autobiography*.[22] When a young woman in our congregation died tragically and I dealt with our loss in a sermon, I turned to these two passages from Barclay's book.

> I believe that pain and suffering are never the will of God for his children. In the days when I was the pastor of people, I could never go into a family where there had been death by accident or where a young person had died too soon and say: "This is the will of God." When these things happen, I am quite certain that there is no one sorrier than God . . .
>
> The lesson of the story [Jesus calming the sea] is that in any storm of life there is the presence of Jesus. The storms Jesus stills are in the hearts of men, so that no matter what tempest of trouble or pain may blow upon life, with him there is calm. Some years ago our twenty-one-year-old daughter and the lad to whom she would some day have been married were both drowned in a yachting accident. God did not stop that accident at sea, but he did still the storm in my own heart, so that somehow my wife and I came through that terrible time still on our own two feet.[23]

For Labor Day Sunday last year I also turned to Barclay. He tells the following story: "I was once present when two men were discussing a house which one of them was contemplating buying. It was a new house. The one named the builder of the house and said to the other: 'You need not hesitate to buy one of so-and-so's houses. He builds his Christianity into his houses.' Here was a builder whose Christianity affected the houses he built."[24]

I've always enjoyed rabbinic stories, so last year, through interlibrary loan, I checked out Martin Buber's two-volume set *Tales of the Hasidim*. I discovered dozens of possible illustrations, several of which have already been mentioned. Here are two others.

A rabbi once asked a peasant, "What would you like best: to get rich, to die old, or to be mayor?" "Rabbi," said the peasant, "that all sounds pretty good."[25]

Soon after the death of Rabbi Moshe, Rabbi Mendel of Kotzk asked one of his disciples, "What was most important to your teacher?"

The disciple thought and then replied, "Whatever he happened to be doing at the moment."[26]

Of course, many other examples could be given of nonfiction books which offer illustrative materials. Books of fiction, however, also offer great possibilities.

I recently read Camus's *The Plague*. While preaching a sermon on our need for human relationships, I turned to a passage from this novel.

"And he, Rieux, thought it too: that a loveless world is a dead world, and always there comes an hour when one is weary .. of one's work, and of devotion to duty, and all one craves for is a loved face, the warmth and wonder of a loving heart."[27]

Years ago, I read John Steinbeck's classic *The Pearl*. An overview of the story provided a powerful illustration about the dangers of materialism.

One of my favorite writers is Garrison Keillor. In his novel *Lake Wobegon Days*, he told about the death and funeral of his pet cat, Pinky. When I preached on James 4:13-15, I told Keillor's story about burying Pinky. The text reads: "Come now, you who say,'Tomorrow we will go into such and such a town and spend a year there and trade and get gain'; whereas you do not know about tomorrow. What is your life? For you are a mist that appears for a little time and then vanishes. Instead you ought to say,'If the Lord wills, we shall live and we shall do this or that.'"

Keillor concluded his story about the death and funeral of Pinky this way:

> Then we stood around the hole, put the cover over Pinky, set the box in the hole, and knelt, gently pushing handfuls of dirt over him. We patted the dirt into a mound and laid a half-slab of sidewalk on it, and wrote, in orange crayon, "PINKY our cat 1950 A.D. We love you. R.I.P." and went in and had macaroons and grape nectar on the porch. We sat in a circle and conversed as people do after funerals. "How is your mother?" I asked Marlys. "She is fine, thank you," she said. "Is your family planning a vacation this summer?" "Yes, we plan to visit the Black Hills in August, Lord willing." "Lord willing" was a phrase learned in church, denoting the uncertainty of the future. It seemed appropriate after burying a cat.[22]

Sermons

While a student in college, I attended many ministerial alliance meetings. (This was required if you wanted to continue receiving your ministerial student scholarship!) At one of the meetings an experienced pastor explained to us his method of preaching. One of the students asked him, "Where do preachers get enough ideas to keep preaching week after week?" Without missing a beat, he said, "You steal."

This preacher was not advocating stealing other people's entire sermons and preaching them week after week. But he did say that other preachers' sermons can be a tremendous source of ideas and illustrations. I have found this to be true in my experience.

Whenever I listen to someone preach, I always take

paper and pencil. If a good illustration is told, I jot it down for later use.

About a year ago, I heard a preacher tell the following story at a senior adult conference. It helps illustrate that church folks are real people and that it's good to laugh. His theme was, "A merry heart doeth good like a medicine" (Prov. 17:22, KJV).

A pastor was out visiting one afternoon. He stopped to see one of the senior adult women in his church. He knocked on the door and heard a noise inside, but nobody answered the door. So he left his business card at the door and wrote Revelation 3:20 on it. That's the verse which says, "Behold I stand at the door and knock; if any one hears my voice and opens the door, I will come in to him."

That night was Wednesday night prayer meeting. The lady he had tried to visit that afternoon attended church that evening. "I missed you today," the pastor said.

"Thanks for leaving the Scripture passage," she responded. "I thought I'd bring you one as well." She then handed him a card which had Genesis 3:10 written on it and walked away. He couldn't wait to look it up. After everybody was gone, he opened his Bible and read the verse. It said, "I heard the sound of thee in the garden, and I was afraid, because I was naked; and I hid myself."

At a seminary luncheon I heard Wayne Oates speak about grief. He told a story about Martin Luther, the great Reformer. A friend of Luther's once wrote him a letter. His wife had recently died, and he was devastated with grief. He asked for Luther's advice. Luther told his friend to grieve, grieve, and then grieve some more. But he warned him finally to put an end to his grief lest he become idolatrous and worship the dead instead of the living Lord.

At a conference on the Christian family, I heard a

preacher tell the following story. I used it soon thereafter when I preached on maintaining a healthy marriage.

This preacher said he grew up with the myth that if a couple loved Jesus and went to church regularly they would never have serious marital problems. That myth began to be shattered as he saw couple after couple in his church go through the agony of divorce. Then his associate pastor divorced. The news crushed the entire church.

A deacon came to this pastor and said, "Pastor, if a man of God (referring to the associate pastor) isn't immune from the threat of divorce, tell me—who is?"

The pastor thought a moment and said, "Absolutely nobody." He got into his car, drove home, and said to his wife, "Honey, this could happen to us." They vowed that day to spend less time being successful at church and more time being successful at home.

Although illustrations can be found by listening to sermons, most pastors don't hear many sermons other than their own. On any given Sunday we are preaching a sermon not listening to one. Printed sermons, however, are available to all and provide a constant source of sermon illustrations.

Wayne Dehoney, previous pastor of Walnut Street Baptist Church in Louisville, Kentucky, is a master at finding and using illustrations. I mentioned one of his illustrations in the last chapter. For years, Dehoney's sermons were printed and sent to preachers all over the world. Somebody once sent me a few, and I was so impressed with his illustrations that I back ordered five years of his sermons! Although I haven't yet been able to read many of them, I now have in my file—just waiting to be read—hundreds and hundreds of sermon illustrations from Wayne Dehoney.

There are many sources of printed sermons—individual pastors who mail out their sermons, books of collected sermons, preaching magazines, etc. I enjoy reading the sermons of John Killinger, pastor of First Congregational Church of Los Angeles. One of his sermons included the following illustration on the love of God demonstrated in the death of Christ. I've learned that it's an old illustration, but it was new to me.

The illustration came from a film Killinger had seen called *The Bridge*. It is the story of a fine young couple who have a son. They are happy together, and the boy is trying to grow up to be just like his father. The film shows the father going off to work. He is the switchman for a railroad line that carries people on holiday from one place to another. Part of the line lies over a river, where it must be drawn back most of the time for boats to pass. It is his job to wait until the last moment, then pull the switch that swings the bridge into place before the thundering approach of the train. We, the viewers of the film, see what the father does not see: His little son has followed him to the river and is coming across the bridge. As the train whistle sounds to signal the approach of the speeding train, the father sees the boy. If he closes the track, the boy will die. If he doesn't, hundreds of people on the train will perish. We watch the agony on his face. He loves the boy better than anything in his life. But finally he pulls the lever and locks the bridge into place. We see the people on the train laughing and having a good time as the train races across the bridge. They do not know how narrowly they have averted disaster or what it has cost the switchman.[29]

When I was working on my series of sermons on the Ten Commandments, I came across the following illustration in another sermon by John Killinger. It helped make the point that the Commandments were given to us by God for our own good. This illustration comes from a novel.

In Sara Orne Jewett's beautiful novel about Maine, *The Country of the Pointed Firs*, she tells about a woman who notices a number of painted wooden stakes scattered about the property of a retired sea captain named Elijah Tilley. She asks Captain Tilley what the stakes mean. When he first plowed the ground, he explained, his plow snagged on many large rocks just beneath the surface. So he set out the stakes where the rocks lay in order to avoid them in the future. Killinger then says that's what the Ten Commandments are all about. God has said: "These are the trouble spots in life. Avoid these, and you won't snag your plow."[30]

Another preacher I enjoy reading is John Claypool. If you are not familiar with him, you might want to purchase one of his several books such as *Tracks of a Fellow Struggler, The Light Within, Glad Reunion* and *The Preaching Event.*[31] His sermon "Working Through Grief" includes the following illustration.

Back around 1800, a child named John Todd was born in Vermont. When he was six, both of his parents died; and the family had to be divided up among various kinfolks. He was sent to live with a maiden aunt whom he had never seen before. She took care of him tenderly and saw him through college and into his chosen profession. Word came to John after he was a grown man that this aunt was about to die and was in terror of this prospect. Since he could not go to be with her personally, he wrote these words to her:

> It is now nearly 35 years since I, a little boy of six, was left quite alone in the world. I have never forgotten the day

when I made the long journey to your house in North Killingsworth. I still recall my disappointment when instead of coming for me yourself, you sent your hired man Caesar to fetch me. And I can still remember my tears and anxiety, as perched on your horse and clinging tightly to Caesar, I started out for my new home. As we rode along, I became more and more afraid and finally said anxiously to Caesar, 'Do you think she will go to bed before we get there?' 'Oh, no,' he answered reassuringly, 'she'll sure stay up for you. When we get out of these here woods, you will see her candle shining in the window.' Presently we did ride out into a clearing, and there, sure enough, was your candle. I remember you were waiting at the door, that you put your arms around me, that you lifted me down from the horse. There was fire on your hearth, a warm supper on your stove. After supper, you took me up to bed, heard my prayers, and then sat beside me until I dropped asleep. You undoubtedly realize why I am recalling all these things. Some day soon God may send for you, to take you to a new home. Don't fear the summons, the strange journey, the dark messenger of death. At the end of the road, you will find love and welcome; you will be safe, there as here, in God's love and care. Surely He can be trusted to be as kind to you as you were to me years ago.[32]

One of the best illustrators I know is Brian Harbour, pastor of Immanuel Baptist Church, Little Rock, Arkansas. His books include *Famous Couples of the Bible, Famous Parents of the Bible, Famous Singles of the Bible, A New Look at the Book, Rising Above the Crowd,* and *From Cover to Cover.*[33]

Harbour also has a monthly sermon service called "Brian's Lines."[34] He will send you a sample copy if you write and ask for one.

All of Harbour's preaching materials are chock full of

usable illustrations. Brian is especially good at finding humorous illustrations. Two follow.

A wealthy Easterner wanted to outdo his Texas cousin in sending a gift to their grandmother. He purchased a zirkah bird that could speak five languages and sing three operatic arias. He paid $25,000 for the unique animal and sent it to his grandmother. The day after Christmas he called her. "Grandmother," he asked, "how did you like the zirkah bird?" "It was delicious," she responded.[35]

After many years of marriage, when childbearing prospects had been about given up, a couple had a son. The pregnancy was such a huge surprise that the mother cried out, "It's fantastic!" Therefore, the boy was named "Fantastic." In due time, the boy grew up, married, and in later years of his life requested that his wife not put the name Fantastic on his tombstone. He explained that he had always disliked the name. When he died, she complied with his request. On the stone she put the dates of his birth and death and this inscription: "In forty years of happy married life he never looked at another woman." And when strangers gazed at his tombstone, they exclaimed, "Fantastic!"[36]

If you are running short of illustrations, try buying several of Brian Harbor's books. You'll soon find a new supply of usable illustrations.

While books of sermons are a good resource for illustrations, you can also find them in preaching magazines such as *Preaching* or *Proclaim*.[37] *Proclaim* is an inexpensive quarterly journal for biblical preaching which features sermon series, individual sermons, illustrations, and articles on the craft of preaching.

Books of Illustrations and Illustration Newsletters

Numerous illustration resources are available for public speakers. While some people discount these as "canned illustrations," they can be helpful.

Several books of illustrations are available for purchase. While these are not my favorite supply of illustrations, they sometimes contain usable material. Take for example, *Knight's Master Book of New Illustrations.*[38] For Easter last year I found in it the following illustration.

Years ago a submarine sank off the coast. As soon as possible, divers descended. They investigated the disabled ship, endeavoring to find some signs of life within. At last they heard a gentle tapping. Listening intently they recognized the dots and dashes of the Morse code. These were the words spelled out, "Is there hope?"[39]

I used the question, "Is there hope?" as the theme of my entire Easter sermon. The story contributed much to my sermon, in spite of its being a "canned illustration."

I used another illustration from this book when I preached on the tongue from James 3. It served as an effective conclusion to the sermon.

A Greek philosopher once asked his servant to provide the best dish in the world. The servant was a wise man. He prepared a dish of tongue. The philosopher asked why tongue was the best dish. The servant said, "It is the best of all dishes, because with it we may bless and communicate happiness, dispel sorrow, remove despair, cheer the fainthearted, inspire the discouraged, and say a hundred other things to uplift mankind." Later the philosopher asked his servant to provide the worst of all dishes. Once again the servant brought a dish of tongue and laid it on the table. The philosopher asked why he brought tongue as the worst of all dishes. The servant said, "It is the worst, because with it we may curse and break human hearts; destroy reputations; promote discord and strife; and set families, communities, and nations at war with one another."[40]

While numerous books of illustrations are available, there are also illustration newsletters. My favorite is *The Pastor's Story File.*[41] Every month this illustration newsletter sends numerous pages of illustrations on a single theme. I've discovered that I am able to use many of their illustrations.

For example, the July 1987 issue was on marriage and family. It included the following story.

A certain man decided to ask his boss for a raise. He told his wife that on Friday he was going to walk into the boss's office and request the raise which he felt he deserved. Naturally, he was nervous and apprehensive. Toward the end of the working day, he finally raised his courage to approach the boss and to his pleasant surprise the employer readily agreed that he was due an increase in salary.

When he arrived home, he noticed the dining room table was set with the best dishes. Candles were burning. His wife had prepared a festive meal. He thought to himself, someone from the office must have tipped her off that he got the raise. He went into the kitchen and told her the good news. They kissed and then sat down to a delicious meal. Beside his plate was a beautifully lettered note, which read: "Congratulations, Darling! I knew you'd get the raise. These things will tell you how much I love you."

They enjoyed the meal together. When she got up to get the dessert, he noticed a second card fall from her pocket. He bent over, picked it up, and read the following message: "Don't worry about not getting the raise! You deserved it anyway! These things will tell you how much I love you."[42]

Another good illustration newsletter is *Windows to Truth*.[43] This resource attempts to find resources which follow the lectionary but is useful even if you don't use the lectionary.

Secular illustration resources may also prove helpful. *Quote*[44] magazine is one example. Here are a few illustrations found in the July 1987 issue.

An on-the-road salesman stopped at a fancy hotel for the night and went to register.

"What are the rates?" he asked.

"A room on the first floor," said the clerk, "is $50. On the second it's $40, and on the third floor, $30.

As the man shook his head and turned to leave, the clerk said, "Aren't you going to register? Don't you find our hotel attractive enough?"

"Oh," said the man. "It's attractive enough. It just isn't tall enough."[45]

This issue, as others, offers numerous quotes on various subjects. From Cullen Hightower comes this quote. "We experience moments absolutely free from worry. These brief respites are called panic." Another one says, "Show me a man who has all his problems behind him, and I'll show you a school bus driver."[46]

Not all the illustrations and quotes are humorous. This same issue quotes Dietrich Bonhoeffer: "The cross of Christ destroyed the equation religion equals happiness."[47]

Magazines and Newsletters

Magazines offer tremendous potential for finding sermon illustrations. Both religious and secular magazines can be used. Anytime you read a magazine, keep your eyes open for possible illustrations. Let me give you one example.

I enjoy reading *Christianity Today*.[48] I read an article some time ago which included the following story. It was an excellent illustration for a sermon on forgiveness.

The illustration came from Simon Wiesenthal's book *The Sunflower*. People often ask Wiesenthal about his obsession with hunting down Nazi war criminals, many of whom are in their seventies and eighties. People ask, Is there no forgiveness available for these people? Wiesenthal answered such questions in his book. He begins with a haunting story, a remembrance of a true event that occurred during his imprisonment.

By chance, Wiesenthal was yanked out of a work detail and taken up a back stairway to a darkened hospital room. A nurse led him into the room, then left him alone with a figure wrapped in white, lying in a bed. The figure was a German soldier, badly wounded, swathed in yellow-stained bandages. Gauze covered his entire face.

In a weakened, trembling voice, the German made a kind of sacramental confession to Wiesenthal. He recounted his boyhood and early days in the Hitler Youth Movement. He told of action along the Russian front and the increasingly harsh measures his SS unit had taken against the Jewish populace.

And then he told of a terrible atrocity when all the Jews in one town were herded into a wooden frame building that was then set on fire. Burning bodies fell from the second floor, and the SS soldiers—he among them—shot them as they fell. He started to tell of one child in particular, a young boy with black hair and dark eyes, but his voice gave way.

Several times Wiesenthal tried to leave the room, but each time the ghostlike figure would reach out with a cold, bloodless hand and beg him to stay. Finally, after nearly two hours, the soldier explained why Wiesenthal had been summoned. He asked a nurse if any Jews still existed; if so, he wanted one brought to his room for a last rite before his death.

"I know that what I am asking is almost too much for you," he said to Wiesenthal. "But without your answer I cannot die in peace." And then he asked for forgiveness for all his crimes against the Jews—from a man who perhaps the next day might die at the hands of this soldier's SS comrades. Wiesenthal stood in silence for some time, staring at the man's bandaged face. At last he made up his mind and left the room, without saying a word. He left the soldier in his torment, unforgiven.[49]

Church newsletters also contain possibilities for illustrations. I receive numerous such newsletters and through the years have found dozens of illustrations, especially in pastors' columns.

Although the following story is probably an old illustration, it was new to me when I read it in a church newsletter. I used it recently in a sermon on the family.

Years ago a man with a Model T was in a state of frustration trying to get his car running again. He had been on the side of the road tinkering with it for hours when another car stopped behind him and the driver offered him assistance. Within a few minutes the car was humming like a sewing machine. "Why that's amazing!" said the man with the now-fixed car. "Where did you learn to fix cars like that?" The gentleman responded: "My name is Henry Ford. I designed this automobile."

I reminded my congregation that God designed the family and gave us principles to follow in order to keep it functioning properly.

One Thanksgiving found my community with little to

be thankful for. Our economy was depressed; people were leaving by the multitudes; and morale was at an all time low. I used the following illustration which was also found in a church newsletter.

An English pastor of years gone by was famous for his pulpit prayers. He always found something to thank God for, even in bad times. One stormy morning a member of the congregation thought to himself, "The preacher will have nothing to thank God for on a wretched morning like this." The pastor began his prayer, "We thank Thee, O God, that it is not always like this."

Newspapers

Karl Barth once advised preachers to keep a Bible in one hand and a newspaper in the other. That's good advice. For one thing, newspapers offer a good supply of illustrations. And since most pastors read a newspaper every day anyway, it's an easy place to find them. I often rip out newspaper articles and place them in my illustration file.

Not long ago I preached on taking responsibility for one's own life. I happened to read about a man who was suing a hospital. A doctor had performed staple surgery on his stomach to help him lose weight. A couple of days after his surgery, he raided the hospital refrigerator and stuffed himself with everything he could find. This tore open the staples and forced another surgery.

He was suing the hospital for having a refrigerator near his room. He claimed the temptation was too great. Thus, his complications were not his own fault but the hospital's fault!

The cartoon section is a good place to look for illustrations. I am preparing a sermon on the importance of listening to our children. In last Sunday's paper,

Dennis the Menace goes to his neighbor's house. He says: "I need somebody who can HEAR me! My Mom is vacuumin' and my Dad is mowin' the lawn."

If you'll be alert as you read the paper, you can find endless illustration ideas. Why not start looking tomorrow morning?

Although the above nine resources don't exhaust all the places to find illustrations, they are a good starting place. Some preachers make up their own illustrations just as Jesus did when He told parables. I've done this a few times but I must admit that I'm not creative enough to do so regularly. I feel like William Barclay when he said, "I've never had an original idea in my life." But by constantly looking for illustrations in the above places, I find I seldom lack for illustrative material. Illustrations abound for the preacher who has the eyes to see and the ears to hear.

Before I conclude this chapter, let me briefly mention one final note. I've spoken of the importance of illustrations, given examples of how they strengthen all parts of the sermon, and mentioned numerous places to find them.

The last issue I want to mention is filing your illustrations. My only real advice is to do it. There are many ways to file illustrations. Find one which works for you and be faithful with it. My method is twofold. First, if an illustration fits a sermon or sermon series I'm collecting material for, I put it in that file. If not, I keep it in an illustration file indexed by subject.

Near the conclusion of the movie *The Wizard of Oz*, the Wizard says something interesting to the Tin Man: "So you want a brain. Where I come from, there are many educated men who have no more intelligence than you. They do have something, however, which you do not have—a diploma." At that point the Wizard gives the Tin Man a diploma, and he begins great feats of mental ability.

Let me apply that story to preaching. Many excellent preachers have no more ability than you. They do have something, however, which you do not—an illustration file! I'm convinced that one of the few differences between an average preacher and a good preacher is a well-stocked illustration file.

At a Lions Club meeting last year, one of my church members complimented my sermon series on the Ten Commandments. He then told me about a conversation he had with his daughter concerning my preaching. "Daddy," she asked, "why does the preacher tell so many stories?"

He replied, "To keep us awake and to drive home the point." Not a bad answer.

Notes

1. Fred B. Craddock, *As One Without Authority* (Nashville: Abingdon, 1983), 68.

2. John W. Drakeford, *Humor in Preaching* (Grand Rapids: Zondervan, 1986), 30.

3. Quoted in a sermon by John Claypool, "The Challenges of Adolescence" September 18, 1977, Northminster Baptist Church.

4. Harold Kushner, *When All You've Ever Wanted Isn't Enough: the Search for a Life that Matters* (New York: Pocket Books, 1986), 171.

5. Hugh Litchfield, *Preaching the Christmas Story* (Nashville: Broadman Press), 32-33.

6. *The Pastor's Story File*, July 1987, vol. 3, no. 9, 4.

7. Martin Buber, *Tales of the Hasidim: the Later Masters* (New York: Schocken Books, 1948), vol. 2, 280.

8. Pearl S. Buck, *The Mother* (New York: Pocket Cardinal, 1965), 198.

9. Cited by Martin Marty in M.E.M.O., *The Christian Century*, November 30, 1983.

10. Buber, vol. 1, 171.

11. Buber, vol. 2, 137.

12. From a sermon by John Killinger, "The Fourth Commandment: Keeping the Sabbath," January 19, 1986, First Presbyterian Church, Lynchburg, VA.

13. *Proclaim*, July, August, September 1987, vol. 17, no. 4, 40.

14. John McBain, *The Ten Commandments in the New Testament* (Nashville: Broadman Press, 1977), 40-41.

15. *Proclaim*, October, November, December 1982, vol. 13, no. 1, 18.

16. C. W. Bess, *Sermons for the Seasons* (Nashville: Broadman Press, 1985), 31-32.

17. Frank H. Seilhamer, *And God Spoke* (Lima, Oh: C.S.S. Publishing Co., 1971), 45.

18. From a sermon by John Killinger, "Jesus' Rules of Order," May 22, 1988, First Congregational Church of Los Angeles, CA.

19. Orville J. Nave, *Nave's Topical Bible: a Complete Analysis of the Bible by Subject* (Nashville: Holman Bible Publishers).

20. Kushner, 165-166.

21. Ibid., 178.

22. William Barclay, *A Spiritual Autobiography* (Grand Rapids: Eerdmans, 1977).

23. Ibid., 51-52.

24. Ibid., 95.

25. Buber, vol. 1, 44.

26. Buber, vol. 2, 173.

27. Albert Camus, *The Plague* (New York: Alfred A. Knoph), 236-237.

28. Garrison Keillor, *Lake Wobegon Days* (New York: Penguin Books, 1986), 159-161.

29. From a sermon by John Killinger, "Why We Still Preach the Cross," May 17, 1987, First Congregational Church of Los Angeles, CA.

30. From a sermon by John Killinger, "The Key to a Good Life: the Real Story of the Ten Commandments," October 6, 1985, First Presbyterian Church, Lynch-burg, VA.

31. John Claypool, *Tracks of a Fellow Struggler* (Waco: Word Books, 1974); *The Light Within You* (Waco: Word Books, 1983); *Glad Reunion: Meeting Ourselves in the Lives of Bible Men and Women* (Waco: Word Books, 1985); *The Preaching Event* (Waco: Word Books, 1980).

32. From a sermon by John Claypool, "Working Through Grief," May 28, 1978, Northminister Baptist Church.

33. Brian Harbour, *Famous Couples of the Bible* (Nashville: Broadman Press, 1979); *Famous Parents of the Bible* (Nashville: Broadman Press, 1983); *Famous Singles of the Bible* (Nashville: Broadman Press, 1980); *A New Look at the Book* (Nashville: Broadman Press, 1985); *From Cover to Cover* (Nashville: Broadman Press, 1982).

34. "Brian's Lines," 11 Oak Tree Circle, North Little Rock, AR 72116.

35. Brian Harbour, *From Cover to Cover*, 190.

36. Ibid., p. 251.

37. *Preaching*, published bimonthly by Preaching Resources, Inc., 1429 Cesery Blvd., Jacksonville, FL 32211; *Proclaim*, 127 Ninth Avenue, North, Nashville, TN 37234.

38. Walter Knight, compiler, *Knight's Master Book of New Illustrations* (Grand Rapids: Eerdmans, 1956, reprinted in 1981.)

39. Ibid., 557.

40. Ibid., 691.

41. *The Pastor's Story File*, Saratoga Press, 14200 Victor Place, Saratoga, CA 5070.

42. *The Pastor's Story File*, July 1987, Marriage/Love/Loyalty vol. 3, no. 9, 3.

43. *Windows to Truth*, P.O. Box 339, Blanco, TX 78606.

44. *Quote: the Speakers Digest*, P.O. Box 3157, Slidell, LA 70459.

45. Ibid., vol. 87, no. 13, July 1, 1987, 199.

46. Ibid., 192.

47. Ibid., 195.

48. *Christianity Today*, 465 Gundersen Drive, Carol Stream, IL 60188.

49. *Christianity Today,* "Are We Asking Too Much?" by Philip Yancey, vol. 29, no. 17, November 22, 1985, 30-31.

4 AUTHORITATIVE PREACH

Years ago ships were the only way communications could be carried from the old countries to America. Anxious for news from relatives and loved ones, people would assemble at the port as soon as a ship was sighted. The moment a gangplank was thrown up and the sailors began to come off the ship, people began to ask: "Is there any word? Is there any word?"[1]

When people come to church today, they, too, want to know, "Is there any word?" They are not that different from the early settlers of America who often felt isolated and cut off from community. They need a word from God for the living of these days. And as ministers of the gospel, we are called to proclaim such a word.

In 2 Timothy 4:2 the apostle Paul exhorted Timothy to "preach the word." Modern-day preachers have that same responsibility. Our sermons ought to be planned, relevant, and engaging. They must, however, be rooted in Holy Scripture. That gives our preaching its authority. As Fred Craddock said, "A sermon that is not directly drawn from Scripture is orphaned, however bright or clever it may be."[2] The authority of Scripture is our only real hope in preaching. If the effectiveness of our sermons depended on our ability and creativity alone, we would be in trouble. The task of preaching, however, is bigger than

103

ourselves. Biblical preaching has life and power far beyond our own feeble attempts to communicate God's Word.

In his autobiography, William Barclay told about his preacher friend A. J. Gossip. Barclay said that Gossip lived closer to God than any man he had ever known. He once heard Gossip tell about a difficult week when he had little time to prepare his sermon. "You know the stair to the pulpit in St. Matthew's?" said Gossip to Barclay. "You know the bend on the stair? Jesus Christ met me there. I saw him as clearly as I see you. He looked at the sermon in my hand. 'Gossip,' he said to me, 'is this the best you could do for me this week?' " and Gossip went on: "Thinking back over the business of that week, I could honestly say: 'Yes, Lord, it is my best.' " And said Gossip: "Jesus Christ took that poor thing that Sunday morning and in his hands it became a trumpet."[3]

My friend Frank Clements tells a story from his days as a circuit rider in the Methodist church. He pastored two little churches in the country. He preached at the smaller one at 9:30 a.m., then drove to the second church just in time to preach at the 11:00 a.m. service.

On this particular Sunday, his sermon at the early service just didn't connect. It was one of the worst sermons he had ever preached. The service concluded at 10:30 a.m. and he began the 20-minute drive to his second church. As he drove, he desperately tried to come up with another idea. He did not want to preach that pitiful sermon again. But no inspiration came. When he arrived at the second church, he began to look in his file for an old sermon he could preach again. As he was looking, however, the organist began the prelude for the service. He was out of time. "This sermon is all I have to offer," he said to himself; and he went into the sanctuary.

Once again, the sermon flopped. After the service was over, Frank walked to his office to throw the sermon into the trash can and to try to forget his failure. As he came to his office, however, a woman stopped him. "Brother Frank," she said, "that sermon was for me." Although surprised, Frank asked her what she meant.

Over the next hour, Frank listened to this woman tell her story. Her husband was in Vietnam at the time, and she was struggling with her two teenage children. Her son had recently been involved in an automobile accident while under the influence of illegal drugs. She just discovered that her 16-year-old-daughter was pregnant. Besides this, the woman was dealing with problems of her own. She had been in deep depression for several months and had become suicidal. She told Frank: "Something inside of me told me to come to church this morning. Your sermon today gave me new hope. It saved my life."

Frank's sermon, pitiful as it was, became God's instrument of hope for a struggling woman. It didn't solve all her problems, but it did give her hope for living. And through careful follow-up, Frank was able to provide significant ministry for this woman and her family. Frank learned something that day about the power of the gospel even when poorly proclaimed.

Almost all preachers are dedicated to preaching the Bible. We don't need to be convinced that we should preach the word. What we need are some ideas for doing it more effectively. That's the purpose of this chapter. I will share with you seven methods for doing biblical preaching. I'll review each of these methods and illustrate them with several examples.

Preaching a Single Sermon from a Specific Text

This is probably the most common form of biblical preaching. The preacher finds a specific passage and preaches a sermon directly from the text.

A few weeks ago, I preached a sermon like this from Mark 14:32-42. This text deals with Jesus' struggle in the Garden of Gethsemane. I called the sermon "Strategies for Surviving Stress." In this passage Jesus was facing the most stressful experience of His life. His response models for us an effective method for dealing with anxiety.

Verse 33 tells us that Jesus was "greatly distressed and troubled." Time was running out for Christ. He was facing the reality of death and was under a tremendous amount of stress.

All people experience stressful times. The question is not whether we'll have stress but how we'll we cope when it comes. In this text we find that Jesus used at least four strategies in dealing with His stress. These same strategies can be applied to our lives.

First, Jesus paused. In verse 32, we read, "And they went to a place which was called Gethsemane." Gethsemane was a grove of olive trees on the Mount of Olives. It was a place of withdrawal and rest for Jesus and the disciples, a place to pause from the stressors of life. Jesus went to it often. In Luke 22:39, the Bible says, "And he came out, and went, as was his custom, to the Mount of Olives." In John 18:2, we discover that "Jesus often met there with his disciples."

Jesus' ministry was stressful. To survive He needed times of rest, times when He could pause from His busy schedule. The Garden of Gethsemane was a place He could do that. And if we are to survive the stressors in our lives, we, too, need to pause.

Baker James Cauthen once said: "Divert daily. Withdraw weekly. Abandon annually."[4] Everybody needs to pause from time to time. All of us need our own Garden of Gethsemane. I mentioned to my congregation various ways we, like Jesus, can take time to pause and how important it is to do so.

The second way Jesus dealt with His stress was by sharing it with people whom He loved. In verse 33, we read, "And he took with him Peter and James and John." And in verse 34 Jesus said to them, "My soul is very sorrowful, even to death; remain here, and watch."

Jesus was facing the most stressful experience of his life. He needed the presence, support, and encouragement of special people. Peter, James, and John were His closest friends. He shared His stress with them.

If we are to survive stress, we need others to help us. We cannot face the stressors of life alone and overcome them. No one is self-sufficient.

As a pastor, I talk to a lot of people who are experiencing stress. Mostly, I just listen to them. After the visit people often say to me, "I feel much better." I wish that happened because I am such a skilled counselor. But that's not the case. People feel better because they have shared their stress with another person who cares about them. One of the keys to surviving stress is sharing it with others. Doing so will help us cope. It will encourage and support us.

A tragedy came to my state a few months ago. A well-known police chief was accused of wrongdoing; and, as a result of the publicity and damage to his reputation, he killed himself. A person who knew him was interviewed on television. He said, "If there had been someone to

whom he could have talked, he would still be alive."
Sharing stress with others is essential.

How did Jesus deal with stress? First, He paused.
Second, He shared His stress with people. And third, He
prayed. In verse 35, we read, "And going a little farther,
he fell on the ground and prayed."

Prayer will help us survive stress. Everybody would
agree with that. But how does prayer help? It's certainly
not a magic formula or cure-all. Prayer does not
necessarily remove the stressors. Jesus prayed for His
cup to pass, but it did not. The apostle Paul prayed for
God to take away his thorn in the flesh, but God did not.

Prayer, however, does help us cope with stress. If
nothing else, it serves as a release. As we share our stress
with a loving God, we find tremendous emotional release
from anxiety.

Prayer also gives us resources to face our stress. That
was Jesus' experience. God did not remove the cup but
gave Him the strength to face it. Like Paul, Christ
discovered that God's grace was sufficient.

Prayer can also be a time of reflection. Through prayer
we can see the stressors in a different light, perhaps even
as beneficial.

And finally, God may hear our prayers for relief and
remove the stressors. However God chooses to respond,
prayer is an important resource for dealing with stress.

So far, the text suggests three ways Jesus coped with
stress. He paused; He shared His stress with people; He
prayed; and finally, He pressed on.

In verse 41, Jesus said, "The hour has come." In verse
42, He said, "Rise, let us be going; see, my betrayer is at
hand." Jesus did not run away from His problems but
faced them head-on.

Ultimately, we must face our stress. We need to pause.

We need to share our concerns with people. We need to pray. But finally we must face our stressors and deal with them directly.

That was Jesus' way. He didn't run away from the mob. He knew He must face them as well as His own death. He came face-to-face with the stress of death, and He pressed on toward it.

Robert Frost once said, "The best way out is always through." This is certainly true when dealing with stress. We can't run away from our problems, if we want to deal with them effectively. If we have a troubled marriage, we must face it head-on. It might involve seeking professional counseling. If we are in financial trouble, we need to come to grips with it and make some changes in our life-style. If we have medical problems, we need to see a doctor and follow his or her advice. Like Jesus, we must face our stressors and deal with them directly.

The above sermon is but one example of preaching a single sermon from a specific text. Many other examples could be given. I recently preached a baccalaureate service. My text was Mark 10:17-22, the story of the rich young ruler. I focused on verse 21, "Go, sell what you have, and give to the poor, and you will have treasure in heaven; and come, follow me."

This young man had it all—youth, wealth, and power. But something was missing. He had everything except eternal and meaningful life. In this text we find a formula for finding meaning.

First, Jesus told us that the quest for materialism is a wrong path. "Sell what you have," he said. Material possessions will not bring contentment. After warning against a wrong path, Jesus pointed the right way for finding meaning in life. Two suggestions are offered. The first is service. "Give to the poor." We will be happy only if we learn to serve others. Meaning in life is found when we invest ourselves in the lives of other people. The second suggestion is discipleship. "Come, follow me." Ultimate meaning in life is found only by following Jesus Christ in serious discipleship.

This outline, filled in with numerous illustrations provided a biblical sermon for an important occasion. It helps illustrate preaching a single sermon from a specific text. Closely related to this method of biblical preaching is to preach several sermons from a specific text. To that I will now turn our attention.

Preaching Several Sermons from a Specific Text

Sometimes, one sermon cannot adequately capture the meaning of a specific passage of Scripture. In this case you might want to consider preaching a series of sermons from the same text. I enjoy this method of preaching and find it effective.

Earlier in this book, I gave an example of such a series—a three-week series from Ephesians 6:4 on parenting. Many other examples could be offered.

I once heard a pastor preach a five-week series on John 3:16 (KJV). It was a powerful series on one of the most beloved verses in the Bible. He preached a sermon on the greatness of God, ("For God"), a second on the love of God, (so loved the world"), a third on the great gift of Christ, ("that he gave his only begotten Son"), a fourth on faith ("that whosoever believeth in him"), and a fifth on eternal life ("should not perish, but have everlasting life.")

One of the great weaknesses of preaching is that it often tends to be too general. Preaching several sermons from one text allows for more specific treatment and more depth.

I am presently collecting materials on two such sermon series. One will be on the 23rd Psalm, the other on the Lord's Prayer. Those passages have so many insights that one sermon cannot do them justice. By looking at them over a period of several weeks, the full impact of the passage can be developed. At this point, I am planning five sermons for each series. One will be preached in the fall and the other in the spring. In this way my congregation and I will be able to look carefully at two of the most well-known passages in the Bible, one from the Old Testament, the other from the New Testament.

Whenever you come across a text which has more possibilities than one sermon can cover, consider preaching more than one sermon on it. The result will be more specific sermons and a better appreciation of the text.

Preaching Through an Entire Book of the Bible

Some preachers do this on a regular basis. They choose a book of the Bible and preach it verse by verse until they finish the book. I do this regularly on Wednesday evenings. Preaching well-constructed, individual sermons with this approach, however, is difficult. While I enjoy this Bible study approach for our casual Wednesday evening service, I haven't used it much for Sunday morning worship.

This method, however, does offer some good benefits. It forces the preacher to deal seriously with the text. It results in biblical preaching. It allows the congregation to become familiar with an entire book of the Bible. It is a good discipline for both preacher and congregation. For these reasons and more, I have recently been doing more of this kind of preaching.

Preaching through an entire book is easier if you'll

choose a short book. I recently did this with the Book of James. I'm preparing now to preach through the Book of Jonah.

Another variation of this method is to preach throughout a book but only from selected passages. You could take a longer book, perhaps one of the Gospels, and preach through most but not all of the passages. I plan to preach through the Gospel of John this way during next year's Sunday evening services. If you have not done this before, perhaps you should consider experimenting with this approach.

Preaching Thematically from a Book of the Bible

In this approach the preacher preaches on the major themes of a particular book. I've done this with several books including Job, Ecclesiastes, 1 Corinthians, Acts, Genesis, and others.

In this method of preaching, no attempt is made to cover the entire book. The goal is to look for a major theme (or themes) and develop sermons around these themes. I'm presently collecting materials from a thematic series on the Book of Philippians. The central text for the series will be 4:11: "I have learned, in whatever state I am, to be content." The title for the series will be, "The Secret of Contentment."

By studying the Book of Philippians, one begins to understand how Paul, in spite of all his problems, was content. Even in prison he was able to affirm his basic satisfaction with life. Most people would like to experience that kind of contentment. The Book of Philippians gives us some clues on how he attained it. By studying this book, I've noticed six such clues. Although I may not preach all of them in the series, listed below are all six possibilities. If you like alliteration, you'll like this series. All points start with the letter P!

Paul had a purpose to live for.—In verse 1:1 Paul called himself a servant of Jesus Christ. His overall purpose in life was to serve Christ. Philippians 3:4-14 further develops this theme. To be content people need a sense of purpose. As one person said, "If you would make someone happy, give them a purpose and the harder the better."

I read once about a couple who adopted a teenage daughter. They gave her everything money could buy, but she remained despondent. A few months later the mother became seriously ill. The adopted daughter had to take over almost all the household chores and help nurse her sick mother back to health. Her parents noticed a remarkable change in the girl. For the first time in her life, she felt needed. She had a cause for which to live. She became vibrant and happy as a result. People need purpose in their lives. Serving Christ was Paul's purpose and is one reason he was content.

Paul knew the presence of God.—In 4:9, Paul said to the Philippians, the "God of peace will be with you." In verse 23, he said, "The grace of the Lord Jesus Christ be with your spirit." Paul experienced this presence of God in his life. It gave him strength to face whatever came. In verse 13, he was able to say, "I can do all things in him who strengthens me." The presence and power of God was with him in all his activities. This helped him be content even in difficult circumstances.

Paul had a positive attitude.—In verses 4-9, we learn much about Paul's basic attitude toward life. He refused to dwell on the negatives. Instead, he majored on the positives. In verse 8, Paul said, "Finally, brethren, whatever is true, whatever is honorable, whatever is just, whatever is pure, whatever is lovely, whatever is gracious, if there is any excellence, if there is anything worthy of praise, think about these things." This positive orientation toward life helped make Paul content.

Paul experienced the peace of God.—In verse 7, Paul said, "And the peace of God, which passes all understanding, will keep your hearts and your minds in Christ Jesus." Although he could not fully explain it, Paul had an inner peace which came by knowing and trusting God as Heavenly Father.

Several years ago an art gallery sponsored a contest. Artists were to paint pictures on the theme of peace. The judges finally narrowed it down to two pictures. One was a beautiful lake scene in the mountains. The other depicted a tree branch hanging over a raging waterfall. On the branch was a nest where a robin comfortably rested. The judges finally choose the waterfall scene as the winner because it illustrated peace in the midst of turbulent surroundings. That is the kind of peace Paul experienced through faith in Christ.

Paul was involved in the lives of people.—In 1:3-11, we read about his special relationship with the people in Philippi. Paul said in verse 7, "I hold you in my heart." He was also close to young Timothy. In 2:22, he said he felt like a father to Timothy. In verse 25, he spoke of his special friend Epaphroditus.

People need people. Paul was blessed with many friends. No person will ever be content alone. God said, "It is not good that the man should be alone"(Gen 2:18). By having people in his life whom he loved and who loved him, Paul was able to be a contented man.

Finally, Paul had a promise of eternal life.—This theme is developed in 1:19-26. Paul said in verse 21, "For to me to live is Christ, and to die is gain."

All of us are going to die. But if we know Christ, we can

have hope even in death. We belong to Him who said, "I am the resurrection and the life, he who believes in me, though he die, yet shall he live." And when we die the Bible tells us that we shall go to a place where "God shall wipe away all tears from their eyes and there shall be no more death, neither sorrow nor crying, neither shall there be any more pain: for the former things are passed away"(Rev. 21:4, KJV).

What were Paul's secrets of contentment? He had a purpose to live for; he knew the presence of God; he had a positive attitude; he experienced the peace of God; he was involved in the lives of people; and he had a promise of eternal life. These factors allowed Paul to be content regardless of his external circumstances.

Although I'm still collecting illustrations and other resources for this series and am not sure what the final outcome will be, I'm looking forward to preaching this thematic series from the Book of Philippians.

First-Person Sermons

Preaching first-person sermons on the great personalities of the Bible is a challenging and effective method of proclamation. Although I don't do this often, it is one my favorite methods of preaching. You simply take on a character of the Bible and tell his or her story.

Several things need to be kept in mind when doing this kind of preaching. First, it should not be done often, perhaps only once or twice a year. If done too often, it will lose its effectiveness. Second, it requires careful preparation. It almost has to be done without notes. Third, while a costume is not required, it usually enhances the sermon.

I included an example of such a sermon in the appendix of my previous book, *Getting Ready for Sunday: a*

Practical Guide for Worship Planning. That sermon was based on Jesus' washing of the disciples' feet. The story is told by the apostle John. I recently did a first-person sermon on Joseph of the Old Testament. The story of Joseph is interesting and lends itself well to a first-person sermon. I introduced myself as Joseph and told my story: being sold into slavery, the experiences in Potiphar's household, being a prisoner in jail, a leader of Egypt, and finally meeting up again with my family. The sermon's primary purpose was to challenge people to be like Joseph and make the best of difficult circumstances. The sermon reminded people that God can bring good even out of bad experiences as illustrated by the story of Joseph.

Although you can write your own first-person sermons, you can also find them in various books and preaching magazines. I have several in my library including *Dramatic Monologue Preaching* and *He Dwelt Among Us.*[5]

Topical Preaching

Although some preachers make disparaging remarks about topical sermons, I've discovered that they can be both effective and biblical. Some subjects cannot be adequately covered by using just one specific text. This is especially true when preaching on the great doctrines of the Bible or on ethical issues. Sermons on the family are another example. In such cases it is often helpful to use numerous passages which relate to your sermon. Obviously, this method can be abused. Preachers sometimes preach topical sermons which have little biblical basis, but that is no reason to abandon this method of preaching. If done carefully and with integrity, topical preaching can be a useful tool of preaching.

A few years ago, I preached a series of sermons on the family. The first sermon presented biblical principles for choosing a mate. The second explored some of the reasons God created the family. The third reviewed some of the principles needed to have a successful family. The final sermon examined some of the major functions of the family. Although these were topical sermons, they were based solidly on biblical principles. It would have been impossible to preach such a series if I limited myself to only one text per sermon.

A few Sunday nights ago, I preached a sermon called "Dealing with Difficulty." During the week I had encountered numerous people in my congregation who were dealing with various difficulties. Although that is always the case, it seemed to be more pronounced at this particular time. I decided to postpone my scheduled sermon and take up this topic instead.

In preparation for this topical sermon, I looked up "Affliction" in *Nave's Topical Bible*[6] It had thirty pages on this subject. The Bible is no stranger to difficulties. Through this process I found several suitable Scripture passages for my sermon. After studying these passages, I developed the following sermon. Actually, it was just a topical Bible study on the subject of difficulties. I based the study on four major points.

When we study the Bible, we discover that difficulties are prevalent among God's people.—Problems are not unusual; they are not the exception. Rather, they are a part of life which we cannot escape. Several passages illustrate this clearly. In Job 14:1, we read, "Man that is born of a woman is of few days, and full of trouble." John 16:33 says, "In the world you have tribulation." Difficulties are just a fact. We must accept them in a broken world. The Bible and experience teach us that difficulties are prevalent.

Difficulties, however, offer possibilities. A cancer specialist once said: "The discovery that people have cancer does one of two things. Either it makes them meaner, crankier, and more difficult to live with; or it makes them sweeter, gentler, and nobler than ever before. It is all a matter of reaction. People can live triumphantly even when they are dying![7]

Serious difficulties are hard to accept. While we should never sugarcoat the struggles of life, they do offer possibilities for growth, insight, and service. Numerous passages in the Bible support this idea.

In Job 23:10, Job said, "When he has tried me, I shall come forth as gold." In Romans 5:3, Paul said, "We rejoice in our sufferings, knowing that suffering produces endurance, and endurance produces character, and character produces hope, and hope does not disappoint us." In James 1:2, we read, "Count it all joy, my brethren, when you meet various trials, for you know that the testing of your faith produces steadfastness. And let steadfastness have its full effect, that you may be perfect and complete, lacking in nothing."

Difficulties can make us better people. They offer us opportunities for growth. They can make us stronger, more loving, and more mature. I mentioned to my congregation several examples of people they knew who proved this principle true.

In difficulties we can know the presence of God. We don't have to face them alone. Sometimes we may not feel or recognize God's presence, but He's always with us. Hundreds of passages speak to this truth.

In Psalm 23:4, we read, "Even though I walk through the valley of the shadow of death,/ I fear no evil;/ for thou art with me." Psalm 18:6 reads, "In my distress I called upon the Lord; to my God I cried for help./ From his temple he heard my voice, and my cry to him reached his ears." Psalm 55:22 says, "Cast your burden on the Lord, and he will sustain you." Second Corinthians 4:8 says, "We are afflicted in every way, but not crushed; perplexed, but not driven to despair; persecuted but not forsaken; struck down, but not destroyed." The biblical message is that we can know the presence of God in every difficulty.

Finally, the Bible has a promise concerning difficulties. It teaches us that one day all struggles will come to an end. In 2 Corinthians 4:17 Paul said, "For this slight momentary affliction is preparing for us an eternal weight of glory beyond all comparison."

I concluded this topical sermon by telling a story about Edgar Jackson called "The Message of the Maples." Edgar Jackson had a stroke and for a while lost his speech. But he eventually regained it and then moved to a farm near Corinth, Vermont. There he met a writer named Edward Ziegler. Ziegler went to see Jackson because he was experiencing several personal problems. He was a fan of Jackson, had read many of his books, and thought perhaps Jackson might be able to help him with his difficulties.

After they had talked awhile, Jackson took Ziegler out to see his pasture. A former owner had once planted maple trees around the entire three-acre perimeter to avoid digging postholes and setting posts for a fence. He waited for the trees to grow, then strung them with barbed wire from tree to tree, enclosing the pasture.

Jackson and Ziegler looked to see how the barbed wire had affected the trees. Some trees had fully incorporated the wires, eventually growing around them and

continuing upward. Others were twisted and deformed
and had never gotten over the intrusion of the wires into
their tender systems.

Some people, explained Jackson, are like the trees that
grew around the wires and went on with what they had to
do. Others are like the stunted, deformed trees. Their
difficulties have ruined their lives and left them smaller,
meaner, and unhappier.

If we are wise in the way we handle our difficulties, said
Jackson, then we will be able to incorporate them and go
on. Our lives will grow tall and straight and we will live
triumphantly.[8]

The above example is but one illustration of a topical
sermon. It was not based on one text but upon many. Yet
it was a biblical sermon, a relevant sermon, and many
said a helpful one. Topical sermons are one of many
methods preachers can use to "preach the word."

Sermons on Personalities of the Bible

Biblical stories about real people can be an effective
means of communicating important biblical truths. Much
can be learned from the people of the Bible. Since people
are interested in people, these sermons usually claim the
attention of a congregation. The possibilities are almost
endless when you consider the many interesting stories of
people in the Bible.

For the month of January a few years ago, I preached a
series of sermons called "Lessons." I took several
characters from the Bible and developed sermons from
their lives.

The first sermon was called, "Lessons from a King."
The text was 2 Chronicles 1:7-13, and the character was
Solomon. In this story God offered a wish to young
Solomon. Rather than asking for wealth, health, or other

selfish things, Solomon asked for wisdom so he could better lead his country. What Solomon wanted most was wisdom so that he could serve his people. The focus of the sermon was the importance of being a servant.

The second sermon was called "Lessons from a Farmer." The text was Mark 4:1-9, and the character was the unnamed farmer in the parable of the sower and the soil. Rather than focusing on the different soils, I focused on the farmer. In spite of all his bad luck, he continued to sow the seed. The theme of the sermon was the importance of persistence.

The third sermon was called "Lessons from a Slave." The text was selected verses from Genesis, and the character was Joseph. The sermon focused on Joseph's experience as a slave and how he made the best of a bad situation. The major thrust of the sermon was "blooming where we are planted."

I'm presently working on a series of sermons based on biblical personalities which I'll call "Nicknames in the New Testament." I got the idea from a sermon called "What's in a Nickname?" by John Gladstone in Harper and Row's first edition of *Best Sermons*.[9] Gladstone mentioned three disciples in the New Testament who had nicknames—John, nicknamed "The Thunderer"; Peter, nicknamed "The Rock"; and Barnabas, nicknamed "The Encourager." Gladstone shared some tremendous insights in this sermon. If you would like to preach sermons on Bible personalities purchase this book and look up his sermon. My feeling is that it covers too much material for one sermon and could be strengthened by making three sermons out of it.

By the way, Gladstone's sermon isn't the only good idea you'll get out of *Best Sermons*. I've already filed away several illustrations and sermon ideas from this book, and I've only read a small portion of it.

The above seven methods do not exhaust all the possibilities for preaching biblical sermons. They do, however, cover the major ones. One of my goals is to preach regularly from each method. This gives variety to my preaching and keeps me from getting into a predictable rut. Regardless of which methods we use, our ultimate goal is to obey the biblical command to "preach the word."

Years ago a conductor led an orchestra in a rousing performance. After it was over, the audience cheered wildly. The conductor went to the microphone and said, "I am nothing: Mozart is everything." Preaching is authoritative not because of us but because it is rooted in Holy Scripture.

Notes

1. John Killinger, *Fundamentals of Preaching* (Philadelphia: Fortress Press, 1985), 13.

2. *Leadership,* Summer 1987, vol. 8, no. 3, 15. "The Making of a Preacher," an interview with Fred Craddock.

3. William Barclay, *A Spiritual Autobiography* (Grand Rapids: Eerdmans, 1977), 18-19.

4. *Proclaim,* Oct, Nov, Dec, 1983, vol. 14, no. 1, 38.

5. Alton H. McEachern, *Dramatic Monologue Preaching* (Nashville: Broadman Press, 1984, out of print); Frederick B. Speakman, *He Dwelt Among Us,* published by The Third Presbyterian Church, Fifth at South Negley, Pittsburgh, Pennsylvania 15232.

6. Orville J. Nave, *Nave's Topical Bible: a Complete Analysis of the Bible by Subject* (Nashville: Holman Bible Publishers.)

7. From a sermon by John Killinger, "Learning to let go of the Past," March 13, 1988, First Congregational Church of Los Angeles, CA.

8. Ibid.

9. James W. Cox,ed., *Best Sermons,* (San Francisco: Harper and Row, 1988), 74f.

P
R
E
A
5 COMPREHENSIVE
H

Preaching, like eating, must be balanced. I like pizza, but I wouldn't want to eat it every day. I like to preach sermons of encouragement; but if that's all I preached, I would be neglecting the great biblical themes of challenge, judgment, and doctrine. Good preaching must be comprehensive.

The Bible is a comprehensive book. It is balanced in form and message. It has a great diversity of literary forms—history, poetry, stories, letters, prayers, vivid apocalyptic literature, and more. The message of the Bible is also varied—salvation for the lost, encouragement for the discouraged, scathing judgment for the hypocritical, hope for the hopeless, ethical standards for the faithful, doctrinal clarity for the confused, devotional material for nurture and growth, and marching orders for the church. Good preaching, like the Bible it is based upon, must be comprehensive.

To help achieve balance, I divide my preaching into five categories—challenge, comfort, calendar, series, and spontaneous—and I attempt to preach regularly from all five categories.

Most of my sermons fall into one of these five categories. I plan my preaching around them. This chapter will briefly review these five categories and give examples of each.

Challenge

I continually try to challenge my congregation. I remind them and myself of the demands of the Christian faith. This means I preach on such things as commitment, renewal, outreach, missions, evangelism, ministry, ethics, and discipleship.

One area where people need challenging is evangelism. Although most of the people in my congregation are already believers, I feel that it's important to occasionally preach an evangelistic sermon inviting people to Christ. I also preach sermons challenging our membership to share their faith with others.

I recently preached a simple evangelistic sermon from the seventh chapter of the Gospel of John. The title of the sermon was "Who Is This Man?" Every person must grapple with the question, "Who is Jesus Christ?" No question is more important. John 7 is an exciting passage concerning the identity of Christ. It is a good text for an evangelistic sermon.

I began the sermon by referring to the controversial film *The Last Temptation of Christ* , which had just been released. While major problems exist in this film, it did get some people to think about the identity of Christ. I told my congregation that we must know who Jesus is. What we don't know on this subject can hurt us. I followed with a humorous story about a Mexican bank robber named George Rodriguez. George made a career out of robbing Texas banks. Tired of this menace, several Texas bankers joined forces and hired a Texas Ranger to hunt him down and bring back their money.

Unknown to George, the Ranger tracked him down and

followed him across the border to the little Mexican village where George lived. The Texas ranger watched George go into the local saloon and followed him. Before George knew what was happening, the Texas Ranger held a gun to his head and said: "I know who you are, George Rodriguez. Tell me where you hid all that Texas money, or I'll blow your head off!"

Unfortunately, George didn't speak a word of English; and the Texas Ranger didn't speak a word of Spanish. Here they were, two grown men, at a total verbal impasse. About that time, a young Mexican who had observed this entire scene walked up to the Texas Ranger. He said: "Mr. Texas Ranger, sir, I am bilingual. If you would like, I'll serve as an interpreter for you."

The Ranger said, "Tell George Rodriguez to tell me where he hid all that Texas money, or I'll blow his head off."

The interpreter immediately gave George the message. With a frantic look on his face George said: "Please tell the big Texas Ranger not to shoot! I haven't spent any of the money. If he will go to the well at the center of town and take ten steps to the north, he will find a big rock. Under the rock he'll find every penny I stole. Tell him quick before he shoots me!"

As the interpreter prepared to give this message to the Ranger, two thoughts came to his mind. First, he thought about all that money under the rock. Second, he thought about the fact that the Texas Ranger had not understood a word of what George said. Finally, he said to the Texas Ranger: "George Rodriguez is a brave man. He says he is ready to die!"

If only George had known English! If only the Texas Ranger had known Spanish! What we don't know can most definitely hurt us. This is especially true when it comes to the identity of Jesus Christ. At this point I turned to the text and began the body of my sermon. I outlined the sermon around three simple questions: (1) What did others say about Jesus? (2) What did Jesus say about Himself? (3) What do we say about Jesus?

What Did Others Say About Jesus?

The people in this story had diversity of opinions concerning the identity of Jesus. His own brothers "did not believe in him" (v. 5). Some said, "He is a good man," while others said, "He is leading the people astray" (v. 12). Many in the crowd marveled at Jesus' teaching and asked, "How is it that this man has learning, when he has never studied?" (v. 15) Some people thought he was crazy. They said, "You have a demon!" (v. 20). Some, however, were asking the big question, " Can it be . . . that this is the Christ?" (v. 26) The religious leaders considered Him dangerous and wanted Him arrested (v. 32). A few people said, "This is really the prophet" (v. 40). Others went further and said, "This is the Christ" (v. 41).

Everyone in the crowd had a different opinion about Jesus. In verse 43, we read, "There was a division among the people over him." Electricity was in the air. People were asking, "Who is this man?" That same question is being asked today.

What Did Jesus Say About Himself?

What the crowd thought about Jesus is interesting, but far more important is what Jesus said about Himself. As we read the entire Gospel of John, we learn that Jesus knew exactly who He was. We catch a hint of His self-identity in verse 29 of this text. Jesus told the people, "I know him, for I come from him, and he sent me." I developed that theme for several minutes, focusing on why God sent Him—to redeem us and to make us whole.

What Do We Say About Jesus?

Finally, I asked the congregation, "Who is Jesus to you?" You will have to answer no more important question in life. I spoke about Jesus' being Savior and Lord of our lives and led into a time of invitation. During the invitation a teenage girl came forward to affirm faith in Christ. She had attended our church for several months and had been grappling with the question, Who is Jesus to me? Although a visible response was made, the sermon had value even if there had been no response. Even longtime Christian believers need to hear the simple story of Jesus.

While preaching evangelistic sermons inviting people to Christ is important, we must also challenge believers to share their faith with others. This past year I preached two such sermons. One was based on Matthew 5:13-16 called "Life-style Evangelism." The other was based on the story of Zacchaeus (Luke 19:1-10), called "Making Friends for Christ."

Evangelistic preaching is just one way to preach sermons of challenge. We also need to challenge our congregation in the area of ethics. Part of our calling to "preach the word" means preaching prophetic sermons on ethical issues of our time. I've preached sermons on peacemaking, ecological stewardship, race relations, world hunger, and other moral issues. While this can be controversial and difficult, it is a vital part of a comprehensive preaching schedule.

We must also challenge our congregation to deeper levels of commitment to Christ and His church. Sermons need to be preached on loyalty, discipleship, stewardship, and service.

Although this kind of preaching is important, it can be overdone. Zealous to see their church more committed to Christ, some preachers challenge their people so much they neglect other important needs.

A few nights ago I went outside to get the newspaper. When I returned, I smashed my bare toe on the leg of the kitchen table. Hurting, I began to moan in pain. About that time my four-year-old came to the kitchen. I thought she had come to comfort me, but instead she said, "Get me some cheese."

Preachers are sometimes guilty of doing the same thing. Our people often come to church on Sunday morning hurting and wounded and struggling. What they need is encouragement and comfort. What they often hear, however, is "Get me some cheese." We challenge them to witness, visit, pray, attend, serve, give money, and be faithful. We need to do this, but we must not do it all the time. To do so is to get out of balance in our preaching and to neglect the needs of our congregation. Preaching must be balanced.

Comfort

God's people also need to hear sermons of comfort. All of us face difficulties and get discouraged. Every Christian has times of struggle, doubt, pain, and crisis. I often bring a word of encouragement, comfort, and hope to my congregation. The Bible has many such passages, and preaching is not complete without it.

Last year after our Easter morning worship service, a woman in our church who was struggling with several serious problems said to me, "I know it's Sunday, but it feels like Friday." Her struggle is shared by millions of people across our nation. People want to celebrate the resurrection of our Lord but sometimes only experience

His cross. As preachers of the whole gospel, we need to be sensitive to this. We are called to challenge our people but also to comfort them. A significant portion of our preaching ought to be sermons of encouragement. And we don't have to look far to find such passages in the Bible; it's full of them.

People need messages of hope and encouragement because life brings much pain and discouragement. Tragedy often comes into our life. We fail in many ways. Relationships crumble. Illness, death, and other bad news comes regularly. Despair and disappointment are common. Darkness often hovers over us and the people in our church. In the midst of such darkness, the Bible offers messages of support, encouragement, and hope. A little girl once asked, "What was God doing last night during the storm?" Then she answered her own question by saying, "Oh, I know, He was making the morning!"[1]

God is in the business of making the mornings. He is a God of hope and strength and light. The people who sit in our churches week after week need to be reminded of that on an ongoing basis.

The Bible is full of passages which comfort: the promise of grace and forgiveness for our failures, the promise of God's presence and strength for our difficulties, and practical advice on how to deal with various problems. This and much more are found between the covers of the Bible. The creative preacher will work hard to incorporate such sermons into his preaching schedule.

Numerous examples have already been mentioned in previous chapters. Several others will come later. At this point, therefore, I will illustrate with just one specific example.

Several months ago, several tragedies hit my community all at once. Four people were killed in automobile accidents within nine days, a young pastor's wife was diagnosed with leukemia, and several people in our congregation were struggling with serious problems. All of these people were good folks. All of them were people of faith. It just didn't seem fair. My sermon on Sunday morning took me to Psalm 73. The title of the sermon was "When Life Is Unfair." The outline for this sermon came from Warren Wiersbe's book *Meet Yourself in the Psalms.*[2] The entire sermon follows.

WHEN LIFE IS UNFAIR

Psalm 73
Preached at First Baptist Church Fordyce, Arkansas July 1988

Fairness is a major issue for children. When something happens to them that seems less than just, you can count on their saying, "That's not fair!" For many years I've listened to my own son regularly remark, "That's not fair!" When he wanted a pet and his mean parents said no, he responded with, "That's not fair."

Through the years I've developed a response. Whenever he says, "That's not fair," I say, "Jonathan, life is not fair." A few months ago, he did something I didn't like and I said, "Jonathan, that's not fair."

He replied, "Papa, life is not fair." Be careful what you tell your children; they may use it against you!

But it's not, is it? Life just isn't fair. Four people in our community died in car accidents this week, including eight-year-old Hunter. We also learned that Lynda has leukemia. Bash is about to die in a Little Rock hospital. Many others among us are struggling. Life is unfair.

And that's the subject of today's text. The psalmist dealt with this difficult subject. He helped answer the question, What do you do when life is unfair? Let's look again at Psalm 73.

1. He Looked Back.

In verse 1, the psalmist said, "Truly God is good to the upright, to those who are pure in heart." This is a great affirmation of faith. The psalmist had been taught from childhood that if he would work hard, worship regularly, and live a moral life, God would bless him. God blessed the good, and God punished the wicked. He believed that living a good life would have good results. Have faith, be moral, and all will go well for you; this was his tradition, his past understanding. But it presented a major problem.

2. He Looked Around

The problem is that he looked around. And when he looked around, he realized that his theology didn't square with his experience.

First, he noticed that bad people often prosper. Judgment didn't come their way; they did extremely well. (see vv. 2-12.) Sinful people enjoyed prosperity, good health, and popularity. Where was justice? These people were arrogant sinners, but God didn't judge them.

Then he noticed that good people often struggle and hurt, including himself (see vv. 13-14). I've been moral and good and faithful to God, but what has it done for me? Nothing—I'm stricken, struggling, and hurting. Where is the justice in the world? Life is not fair.

I can relate to the psalmist's feelings. I am bothered when I see evil, mean, and unethical people prosper. And worse than that, good people often suffer. Like Tom, a successful businessman. Tom was a devout believer. He was honest and treated his employees well. He tithed every dime of his earnings, plus some. He loved his family and was a good father. He regularly witnessed and shared his faith with others. A few years ago Tom's business collapsed, and he went bankrupt.

Or what about Bill and Susan? They desperately wanted a child. They tried for years but were unsuccessful. They saw many doctors. They prayed for a child. Then finally, gloriously, Susan became pregnant. Filled with joy, they began to prepare a baby's room. And then one morning Susan woke up feeling ill. She had a miscarriage that evening.

Or what about Jim and Melinda? They had a child. They loved their child and brought him up in a positive, Christian environment. But their son left home, took up with the wrong crowd, and was taking drugs.

Or what about Guy? Guy was a wonderful person, one of the kindest people you'd ever want to meet, as was his wife. They were Christians and deeply loved God and their church. One day while Guy was plowing his field, a storm suddenly blew over. As he tried to get his tractor back to the barn, a lightning bolt struck him dead.

The list goes on and on—like all the fine people in our town who just this week have suffered terrible tragedy. Yes, life is unfair.

3. He Looked Within

The psalmist looked back and remembered his theology—that good people prosper and bad people are judged. But when he looked around, that just wasn't the case. Then he looked within. And that was a struggle.

Look at verses 15-16. The psalmist was struggling. He tried to understand life's unfairness, but it was a wearisome task. It made no sense. It didn't seem right.

I appreciate the psalmist's honesty. He didn't play games. He freely shared his struggle. He was honest with himself and with God. It encourages me to know that even the great men and women of the Bible and in church history struggled with their faith. We need to remember that faith asks these hard questions, not lack of faith. People who don't believe in God and His goodness don't think about these things; they don't have to struggle with such issues. The psalmist was in a faith struggle. And if we are honest, all of us have similar experiences.

Struggling with such issues is a mark of growth and faith. Martin Luther once said, "He who doesn't think he believes, but is in despair, has the greatest faith." Luther was saying that when you struggle with your faith as the psalmist was doing, that's when you have the most faith. Shallow faith doesn't struggle with hard questions; deep faith does.

The psalmist wanted to believe that God is fair and good. But if so, why is life so unfair? Even in his struggle, however, he was a man of faith. He sought help from God in coping with his dilemma. In his search we find some answers which can help us deal with the unfairness of life.

4. He Looked Ahead

After looking back, around, and within, the psalmist looked ahead. He was reminded that what goes around, comes around. (see vv. 17-20). In the future the wicked will be punished, and the righteous will receive their reward. Life may be unfair now, but it won't always be. A day will come when things will be made right. A day of reckoning is coming.

A story is told of two farmers. One was an atheist. He was also immoral and dishonest. The other was a devout Christian. He treated his employees fairly, was a faithful church member, and he never worked on Sunday. The atheist farmer loved to poke fun at the Christian farmer. He regularly ridiculed his faith.

Harvest came and went, and in the month of November the two farmers saw each other at the bank. It had been a good year for the atheist farmer, but the Christian farmer had had a bad year. When the atheist farmer saw the Christian farmer in the bank, he sarcastically made fun of him and his faith. Gloating in his wealth, the atheist farmer said to the Christian farmer: "What good is faith? It hasn't done you any good." As they walked out of the bank, the Christian farmer said to the atheist, "Just remember, God doesn't settle all his accounts in November."

As the psalmist struggled with the fact that evil people do well and good people struggle, God reminded him that in the future all accounts would be settled. Judgment would come upon the wicked, glory and reward on the righteous.

5. He Looked Above

Looking ahead helped some but not enough. Judgment and reward may come in the future, but we live in the present. When life is unfair, how do we cope with it in the here and now?

So after looking back, around, within, and ahead, the psalmist finally looked above. And by looking to God, he found the strength to go on even when life was unfair.

We cannot cope with life's unfairness with our own resources. We need God's help, and He wants to give it. John Bunyan graphically illustrated this in *The Pilgrim's Progress*. An illustration in the book shows an old man with a rake in his hand, bent, and careworn, with his eyes fastened on the worthless things of this world.

Meanwhile, a shining angel stands over his head, offering him a crown. But the man can't see it; he never looks up.

If we would only look up, God is ready to help us. As John Phillips once said: "Psychologists tell us, Look within. Opportunists advise, Look around. Optimists say, Look ahead, while pessimists say, Look out! But the Holy Spirit encourages us to Look up."

Finally, the psalmist looked up to God and found strength to face unfair situations (see vv. 21-28). He didn't find easy answers to his questions of fairness. There are none. But he found something even better—the presence of God. And God's presence will carry us through whatever comes, even through the unfair, hard times of life.

And how do we find God's presence and strength to face and cope with life's unfairness? The psalmist found it in worship. (see vv. 16-17). Only when he went into the sanctuary of God was he able to cope with his struggle. We need worship. And when we don't feel like worshiping, that's when we need it the most. For in worship—corporate and individual—we discover the presence and power of God (see vv. 23-26).

In the end, looking above is the only way to cope with life's unfairness. We'll never understand why good things happen to bad people and bad things happen to good people. But answers aren't what we need anyway. We need strength. We need God's power and presence to face what comes. And the promise of God is that if we'll look up, He will help us.

Conclusion

Let me conclude by telling you about a young woman, who, like the psalmist, struggled with the unfairness of life. A chaplain friend told me about her experience. He ministered to her for several months while she was in the hospital.

Like the psalmist, this woman grew up believing that if you believed in God and were a good person things would go well for you. But they didn't.

After 20 years of marriage, her husband left her; and they got a divorce. Not long thereafter, she lost her house because she couldn't make the payments. And a few months later the doctors discovered that she had terminal cancer.

My chaplain friend walked with her through her long pilgrimage with cancer. Like the psalmist, she began her struggle by looking back. She told this chaplain that she had grown up believing that God would take care of His own. But then she looked around. She saw her divorce, the loss of her home, and now the cancer. These things didn't match up with her past beliefs. So she, like the psalmist, looked within. She deeply struggled. She went through the normal stages of anger and depression. Finally, she came to grips with her imminent death. After a long struggle with her faith, she, like the psalmist, began to look ahead. Death was near, and her belief in eternal life became tremendously important to her.

But this woman also looked above. During the last few weeks of her life, she knew the presence of God in a special way. God didn't take away her pain and struggle, but He entered it with her. Her final goal in life was to see her youngest son graduate from high school. The doctors said it was impossible, but she went anyway. God gave her the strength.

A few days after her son's graduation, she died. This chaplain and many others who worked at the hospital grieved. My chaplain friend told me that this woman changed his life forever. He said, "I've learned through this experience that even when life is unfair, God's presence can be found."

Calendar

A third preaching category is the calendar. Many special days and seasons guide my sermon topics and texts. These include the Christian calendar (Advent, Lent, Palm Sunday, and Easter), the secular calendar (Mother's Day, Father's Day, Labor Day, Memorial Day, Independence Day, Thanksgiving, and New Year's Day), the denominational calendar (Witness Commitment Day, Baptist Men's Day, Senior Adult Day, Day of Prayer for World Peace, World Hunger Day, and Race Relations Day), and the local church calendar (revival preparation, Lord's Supper services, stewardship campaigns, and so forth).

I schedule approximately half of my sermons based on calendar considerations. This is an important part of my planning and helps me develop a comprehensive schedule of preaching. Since this process was described in detail in chapter 1, I will not review it again. To illustrate this category of preaching, I'm including a summary of a sermon I once preached for a Good Friday service.

THE CRUCIFIED GOD

The congregation gathered for a Good Friday worship service, similar to the one we are participating in tonight. This particular service, however, was held at the town's Catholic Church. After music and Scripture readings came the sermon. The preacher, a visiting monk, walked to the pulpit, looked at the congregation but said nothing. After a few moments of silence, he picked up a candle and walked to a statue depicting Christ on the cross. The statue was in a dark corner and could barely be seen in the evening light. The monk lifted the candle to Christ's head, illuminating the crown of thorns. He then placed the candle near the outstretched arms of Christ, shedding light on the nail-scarred hands. Next, he placed the candle near the side of Christ, exposing the wound from the soldier's spear. Finally, he placed the candle at the bottom of the statue so the congregation could see the nail in Christ's feet. With that he blew out the candle and dismissed the service.

To speak of the cross is to speak of suffering. To speak of the cross is to describe a scene of death and brokenness and pain. To speak of the cross, however, is also to speak of God. And that's the surprising thing about Good Friday. When we look at the cross, we see a picture of God—not a God of glory and majesty but a God of suffering. To look at the cross is to see a crucified God.

We know that God is the Lord of power and glory and awesome transcendence. Yet Good Friday tells us He is also a God of suffering. The cross of Good Friday tells us that God suffers for us and that God also suffers with us.

God Suffers for Us

The Scriptures say, "All have sinned and fallen short of the glory of God"(Rom. 3:23). They also warn us that "the wages of sin is death"(6:23). On the cross, however, Christ paid the debt and died in our place. "He was wounded for our transgressions" (Isa. 53:8), says the Bible. "Christ has offered for all time a single sacrifice for sins"(Heb. 10:12).

We cannot understand this, but we do know that it's good news. Christ's death vividly illustrates God's love for us. "For God shows his love for us in that while we were yet sinners, Christ died for us (Rom.5:8). Regardless of our inability to comprehend this sacrifice, Christ died in our place; God suffered for us.

Several years ago a fire broke out in an apartment at one of our seminaries. A young seminarian, his wife, and three children were living in the apartment. Awakened by the smoke and flames, the family rushed out of the house. Somehow, in the wildness of the scene, a mix-up occurred. The father thought his wife had grabbed their baby, and the wife thought her husband had the baby. Only after running outside did they realize the terrible truth—the child had been left inside.

Immediately, the father ran back into the blazing apartment to rescue his little girl. Tragically, he never returned. They both perished in the fire.

The next day the seminary community gathered together for worship. The president of the seminary stood and read from Holy Scripture, "Greater love has no man than this, that a man lay down his life for his friends"(John 15:13).

Jesus laid down His life for you and me. Like this young seminary father, He sacrificed everything for those He loved. This is a great mystery. But through Christ's suffering we can know forgiveness and new life. God is a crucified God. God suffers for us.

God Suffers with Us

Not only does the cross affirm that God suffers for us, but it also says that God suffers with us, that He understands our suffering and enters into it with us.

We live in a world of suffering. None of us are immune from struggle. Good Christian people often experience serious problems. The cross, however, says that God is present with us in the midst of our struggles. It tells us that God suffers with us, that we are not alone with our wounds.

Elie Wiesel, a survivor of the Nazi holocaust, tells a story from his experience in a concentration camp which can illustrate God's presence in human suffering.

In his book *Night*, Wiesel described a hanging at Buna, a camp near Auschwitz in the southern part of Poland. The three victims, one of them just a youth, had been accused of blowing up a power station. In order to warn the other inmates of the high cost of resistance, all the inmates were forced to walk by and see the execution at close range.

It was a grisly scene, a scene of death, evil, and suffering. By the time Wiesel marched by, the two adults were dead. But the youth was still alive, hanging on the gallows, struggling between life and death.

Behind him Wiesel heard a man ask a question: "Where is God now? Where is He?"

That's the question, isn't it? Where is God? Where is He in my illness? Where is He as I face the reality of death? Where is God as I face a deteriorating marriage, financial problems, doubt, and depression?

The execution continued. The lad lingered on. "Where is God now? Where is He?"

And Wiesel wrote: "And I heard a voice within me answer him: 'Where is He? Here He is—He is hanging here on the gallows.' "[3]

God does not take away all our suffering. But He does enter into our pain and shares it with us. God is no stranger to struggle. The cross tells us that. Jesus is indeed "a man of sorrows, and acquainted with grief." The cross tells us that God suffers with us. He is present in all our struggles.

That's the promise of God throughout the Scriptures.

As the psalmist said, "Though I walk through the valley of the shadow of death, I will fear no evil; for thou art with me"(Ps, 23:4).

We don't always remember that. Sometimes God's presence is hard to find. Even Jesus struggled with this. On the cross He cried, "My God, my God, why hast thou forsaken me?"(Matt.27:46) And yet, a few moments later, He was able to say, "Father, into thy hands I commend my spirit"(Luke 23:46, KJV).

It is no accident that the last words of Christ recorded in the Gospel of Matthew are, "Lo, I am with you alway, even unto the end of the world" (28:20, KJV). And His presence is always with us, even in suffering.

And so on this Good Friday we look again at the cross. And once again we see a God of suffering—a God who suffers for us and a God who suffers with us.

To be sure, this isn't the last word. Sunday is coming. But today is Friday. And Friday is a day to look once again at the cross and to see the crucified God.

(A soloist then sang a cappella, "Were You There?" to conclude the worship service.

Series

A fourth area of preaching is special series. I often preach a series on a particular book of the Bible or on topics of interest and need. I have several series per year as part of my planned preaching schedule.

I enjoy preaching sermon series. In reviewing my sermon file I discovered that I've preached more than 35 such series (including evening services) over the past six years. They range from a short series of two sermons to a 10-week series on the Ten Commandments. Preaching in series helps in annual sermon planning and weekly sermon preparation and makes preaching more interesting. I would highly recommend that you experiment with this kind of approach.

I have already mentioned more than a dozen such series in previous chapters, several in detail. Because of that I will not give many more examples. I will, however, tell you about my most recent series. It's a four-week series called "Keys to Happiness." At this point I've preached two of the sermons, have written the third, and have outlined the fourth. The idea for this series came from a similar series preached by Wayne Dehoney at Walnut Street Baptist Church in Louisville, Kentucky in 1982. Although my sermons are different from his, the basic themes are the same.

Several years ago, while counseling a person who had a lot of problems, I asked, "What do you really want out of life?"

This person responded by saying, "I just want to be happy."

Don't we all! Yet happiness is elusive. It's hard to grasp. So we try even harder to find it. Americans take seriously the "pursuit of happiness."

Most people look for happiness in externals such as material possessions, career advancement, status and power, and education. While externals may help us find some happiness, they are not the real key. We've all known people who have all the right externals—plenty of money, a good job, status in the community—yet are still unhappy.

I'll never forget listening to a speech by a recovering alcoholic. She said her life was one long search for happiness. She tried to find it in her job, in material possessions, in a string of relationships with numerous lovers—yet she could not find happiness. She finally turned to drugs and alcohol and almost destroyed herself.

Fortunately, with the help of Alcoholics Anonymous, she straightened her life out and began to find the happiness she was seeking. She ended her speech by saying: "I've learned that external circumstances cannot and will not bring you happiness. Happiness," she said, "is an inside job."

Some people try to find happiness through a positive mental attitude. They say that if you'll just have a good attitude you'll be happy. Unfortunately, this doesn't always work. I know a man who advocates this positive attitude philosophy. He works hard to be positive. He smiles big, shakes your hand warmly, and says everything is great. But it wasn't great, and I knew it. One day I said to him, "Gary, what's really going on inside of you?" He said, "Martin, I feel as if I'm bleeding to death."

External circumstances and positive attitudes may help people be somewhat happy, but they are not the keys to finding genuine happiness. What then is the secret? How do we find happiness in our lives? I'm coming to the conclusion that happiness is a by-product of other things. It comes indirectly. You can't chase after happiness for itself—it won't work. Happiness is the result of having other things right in your life. And in this series I explored with my congregation what some of those things are.

The series explores four keys to finding happiness: knowing the forgiveness of God, being able to adjust to the changes and problems of life, serving other people, and being a person of gratitude. Although these are topical sermons, each one is grounded in a specific text.

Of the five categories I use for planning my preaching, my favorite is sermon series. The possibilities are almost endless. I'd encourage you to try some for yourself. Listed below are a few of my most recent sermon series.

"Teach Us to Pray"

"This We Believe"

"The Christian and Anger"

"The Seven Last Words of Christ"

"The Ten Commandments for Today"

"Word of God Across the Ages"

"Illness Through the Eyes of Faith"

"The Secret of Life"

"Principles for Parenting"

"Principles for Partnership"

Spontaneous

The last preaching category could be called spontaneous preaching. Sometimes I feel inspired to preach on a particular text or topic. Special circumstances may influence my pulpit planning. These might include a particular crisis or celebration or a special need or contemporary event which needs addressing.

I've already mentioned several such sermons. When a teenage boy in our church was killed in a car accident last year, I postponed my scheduled sermon and preached a sermon from Habbakkuk called "The Just Still Live by Faith."

The sermon in the section on comfort, "When Life Is Unfair," is another example of a spontaneous sermon. It was in response to several tragic events which had just occurred in our community.

A few months ago my mother-in-law was killed in a tragic automobile accident. When I returned to the pulpit, I preached from James 4:13-16. This passage reminds us that we are like a "mist that appears for a little time and then vanishes"(v.14). The title of the sermon was "Tentative and Temporary."

A few years ago our church was a in a dry spell. We decided to have a "Loyalty Day." We asked people to make a special effort to be at church and to bring a generous offering as an act of loyalty. I set aside my planned sermon and put together a topical sermon called "Expressions of Loyalty."

Several years ago the board game "Trivial Pursuit" became popular. One particular week found our community in the middle of a Trivial Pursuit tournament. The whole town was talking about this event. That Sunday morning I preached a sermon on discipleship called "No Trivial Pursuit."

During a special election concerning legalized casino gambling in our state, I preached a sermon called "No Dice to Casino Gambling in Arkansas."

After my grandfather died a few years ago, I set aside my scheduled sermon and preached on "The Hope of Heaven."

Numerous other examples could be given, but they would not be helpful to you. Spontaneous sermons have to come from your own experience. The principle, however, is important. Sometimes you will feel compelled to alter your preaching plan and to preach spontaneously. These sermons have the possibility of being the most effective preaching you'll ever do.

These five categories help summarize various ways of preaching. They give me a handle for organizing my sermons. Their greatest value is to help me achieve balance. They are tools for planning a comprehensive preaching schedule. By planning my preaching around these five categories, I find that I have more sermon ideas than Sundays to preach them.

Notes

1. James W. Cox, ed., *Best Sermons*, (San Francisco, Harper and Row, 1988), 27.

2. Warren Wiersbe, *Meet Yourself in the Psalms* (Wheaton, IL: Victor Books, 1983), 32.

3. Elie Wiesel, *Night, Dawn, Day* (New York: Signet, 1984), 79-81.

```
P
R
E
A
C
```
6 HUMAN

At the age of fifteen, I walked down the aisle of a Baptist church, took the preacher by the hand, and said, "Brother Bill, God has called me to preach." Three weeks later I stood behind the pulpit of that church and preached my first sermon. I was so nervous I thought I was going to wet my pants. Before I knew what I was saying, I actually told the congregation that I was so nervous I thought I was going to wet my pants! The people howled with laughter. I turned bright red, and my preaching ministry was birthed in a very human way.

And that's as it should be. In Acts 14, the people of Lystra tried to make gods of Paul and Barnabas. Paul cried out, " Why are you doing this ? We also are men, of like nature"(v. 15).

Good preaching must be human. We preach a divine message, but it is communicated through human instruments. As the apostle Paul said, "We have this treasure in earthen vessels"(2 Cor. 4:7).

Unfortunately, many ministers are uncomfortable sharing their humanity with their congregations. They try to be different from other people. Charles Spurgeon once said: "Ministers generally have an appearance peculiarly their own. In the wrong sense, they are not as other men are. They are too often speckled birds, looking as if they were not at home among the other inhabitants of the country but awkward and peculiar."

To be authentic and effective, however, a preacher needs to share his humanity with his congregation. Rather than being a detriment to ministry, our humanity can be an asset. Chevis Horne said that a pastor's humanity can be one of his greatest assets. He suggested five benefits of being an authentically human minister. First, it puts us in touch with the reality of our own humanity. Second, it makes us open to the grace of God. Third, it opens us not only to God but also to people. Fourth, it helps us accept ministry from others. Fifth, and most important for our purposes, it makes our preaching more effective. His comments on this subject as follows.

> Next to the grace of God, my humanity is my greatest asset in the pulpit. Only a person who has known the grace of Christ can tell others of that grace. Only a saved sinner can tell other sinners where grace is, where forgiveness can be found. Only those who have been wounded and had their wounds healed can tell others where they can be cured. Only men and women who know they must die, and that all too soon, can exult in the resurrection of Jesus Christ. Only they can preach Easter's message with power.
>
> The truth is the brokenness of our humanity can be like crevices through which the grace of Christ is poured like spring showers on parched and thirsty fields.
>
> My humanity will help me do confessional preaching which is so necessary for vitality in the pulpit. I confess I am a sinner, that I am caught in the sinful structures of my world. There should be those moments when I leave the pulpit psychologically, go into the pew with my people, and make my own confession with them.
>
> If I am to do prophetic preaching that is not disruptive and which allows me to keep my pulpit, I have to do

confessional preaching. If I am willing to confess my own part in the sin of my society and culture, I can then tell my people of theirs and they will not reject me. I tell them of their sin as a confessor, not as judge.[1]

Accepting and affirming our humanity removes the burdens and dangers of trying to be a spiritual superman. When Angelo Roncalli assumed the great burden of the church as Pope John XXIII, he comforted himself at night with this prayer: "But who governs the church? You or the Holy Spirit? Very well then, go to sleep, Angelo."[2]

Accepting our humanity helps relieve many burdens of ministry. We can learn along with Pope John XXIII that we don't have to be God. The church and its problems are not all our responsibility. Affirming our humanity can also save us from the dangers of trying to be more than human.

Captain James Cook, the British explorer, lost his life because he allowed the people of the island of Hawaii to think he was a god. While Cook was in the harbor for the first time, the natives thought he was a deity; and Cook did nothing to discourage them. After accepting their deification, he left the harbor, sailing into a fierce storm where his ship was blown and battered. When he returned to the harbor, the natives were puzzled. How could such fate have overtaken a god? Feeling betrayed, they attacked the ship and killed the captain. The pastor who fails to allow his people to see that he has feet of clay may also be unwittingly responsible for his own demise.[3]

The burdens and dangers of trying to be more than human are not worth the cost. In the end they do not help our preaching but hurt it. Being an authentic human being is an important element in our entire ministry. The subject of this book, however, is proclamation. I will narrow my focus, therefore, to being human in our preaching, especially in the areas of delivery and content.

Sermon Delivery

Being authentically human in our preaching is a liberating experience. This is especially true in the area of sermon delivery. It means God can use us in spite of and even because of our uniqueness, weaknesses, and idiosyncrasies. We can be ourselves in the pulpit and not try to imitate someone else. One of the great temptations for young preachers is to imitate other preachers. This keeps them, however, from developing their own unique styles and stifles their effectiveness.

An old rabbinical story tells about a young rabbi named Noah. When Rabbi Noah's father died, Noah assumed his father's position. Several of his disciples noticed that there were a number of ways in which he conducted himself differently from his father, and they asked him about this. "I do just as my father did," he replied. "He did not imitate, and I do not imitate."[4]

Accepting our humanity means we won't imitate other preachers' preaching styles but develop our own. Although we can learn from other preachers, we are not to copy them. As someone has said, "David cannot fight in Saul's armor."

Every preacher has his own unique style of preaching. Instead of imitating somebody else's style, he needs to master his own. The result will be sermons which are natural and thus more effective.

Being human in our preaching means we can be ourselves. It also means we can preach conversationally. I'm convinced that conversational preaching is the best way to deliver a sermon. This kind of preaching may be animated but not oratorical. It is preaching to people as

you would talk to them in their home. In his book
Preaching for Today, Clyde Fant advocated this kind of
preaching. He said that sermon delivery should be
human, natural, and conversational. "In short," he said,
"preaching should be natural."[5]

Too many preachers take on a totally different style of
speaking when they enter the pulpit. They do not speak
conversationally but take on oratorical manners of
speaking. This does not enhance their preaching but
hinders it.

A young Jewish boy once saw a rabbi praying. Full of
amazement he came running to his father and asked how
it was possible for a rabbi to pray quietly and simply
without giving any sign of ecstasy.

"A poor swimmer," answered his father, "has to thrash
around in order to stay up in the water. The perfect
swimmer rests on the tide and it carries him."[6] The same
thing could be said about preaching.

I have a preacher friend whom I'll call Steve. He is a
warm, charming, and caring person. Talking with him is
a joy. When Steve enters the pulpit, however, he
completely changes his style of speech. The warmth and
spontaneity of his regular, conversational speech is
completely lost; and his preaching suffers because of it.
His voice takes on a sort of whine; he shouts a lot; he
thrashes about in the pulpit; and he speaks with an old-
fashioned, oratorical style. If Steve would preach as he
talks in conversation, his quality of preaching would
greatly improve.

For the life of me, I cannot imagine Jesus preaching
with an oratorical style. Neither can I imagine Jesus
shouting or pounding on a pulpit or thrashing about as
He preached. The gospel does not need to be screamed. I
believe that Jesus spoke with great animation yet in a

conversational style. Most of His preaching was in the form of stories, and good storytelling is done conversationally. The best preachers preach as they talk. That is human preaching, and it is effective.

In his book *Fundamentals of Preaching,* John Killinger spoke to this issue. He said:

> Preach naturally. In former times, many preachers developed oratorical manners of speaking out of sheer necessity: without amplifying systems, something had to be done to increase the projecting power of the human voice. Today, with sensitive and relatively inexpensive amplifiers, there is no need for such affected voices. The ideal of speech is heard in the normal, almost conversational, tones of the evening news broadcast. For preachers to persist in using artificial patterns of inflection and abnormal volume is to mark the church as an anachronistic society, frozen in the never-never-world of some previous era. We should speak to a congregation as we would to an intimate group of friends—raising and lowering the voice naturally, gesturing for emphasis as the body normally moves to sculpt the pictures it is seeing, and generally behaving as though we were sane, healthy, and emotionally sound human beings. That way the gospel is more credible in the age in which we live. It is being heard through our personalities, not through some fabricated personalities that we stand in the pulpit for twenty minutes on Sunday morning.[7]

Sermon Content

The best way to express humanity in preaching is not through sermon delivery but through sermon content. We share our humanity more through what we say than how we say it.

Human preaching means we don't have to have all the

answers. We can be vulnerable with our congregation. It means that we can be, in the words of John Claypool, "a fellow struggler." When we preach in this manner, our congregation can trust us. They know we experience the same joys and struggles they do. A human preacher is a believable preacher. He is heard gladly by his people.

One of the best ways to express our humanity is through humor. A human preacher is able to laugh at himself. By doing so his congregation can better understand and accept his limitations.

Early one morning my wife drove to the grocery store. I was lathering my face with shaving cream when the car returned. I heard a knock at the door. Assuming my wife's arms were full of groceries, I opened the door. I was wearing underwear and shaving cream. To my great surprise it was not my wife. Rather, it was one of the ladies of the church. But not just any lady. It was the president of the Woman's Missionary Union!

When I told this story to my congregation, the roof almost caved in! I wanted them to know, however, that preachers shower and shave like any other man. It was one way to let them know of my humanity.

In his sermon one Sunday morning, my friend Lloyd Anderson said to his congregation, "I know I'm not all you want in a pastor." A few good-natured "amens" were heard across the sanctuary. He paused a moment, stared at the congregation, then said, "But look what I'm stuck with!" The people laughed. They understood the point. They and their pastor were normal human beings with both strengths and weaknesses, and they needed to accept that reality if their church was to be effective in its ministry.

This kind of humor lets people know their pastor is a real person—that he struggles with the same issues they do. It makes him an authentic person, believable and trustworthy.

Humor is only one way to express our humanity in the pulpit. There are many other ways. The important issue is that our congregation know "we are men like themselves."

In his 1838 divinity-school address at Harvard, Ralph Waldo Emerson expressed his disdain for a preacher whose sermon "had not one word intimating that he had laughed or wept, was married or in love, had been commended, or cheated, or chagrined. The capital secret of his profession, namely, to convert life into truth, he had not yet learned." The "true preacher," for Emerson, "was one who deals out his life to the people."[8]

Some of my best preaching experiences have been instances where I openly shared my struggles with my congregation. When my wife's 52-year-old mother died a few months ago in a tragic automobile accident, I spoke openly in a sermon of my anger and grief. I shared what I was learning through this experience by turning to a passage of Scripture which helped inform my experience.

Two years ago, when my grandfather died, I preached a personal sermon on what he had meant to me, how he had influenced my Christian pilgrimage, and how his death made the hope of heaven come alive for me.

I've recently been struggling with a serious throat disorder. It threatens my ability to remain in the pastorate. I've shared this struggle with my congregation. I told them how my faith was helping me through this ordeal. Numerous people mentioned to me that these references to my illness have helped them with their own struggles.

When I have the sad occasion of burying young people who were still in the prime of life, I am honest with my congregation about the pain and questions I'm experiencing. They have learned that asking hard questions isn't a lack of faith but a part of authentic faith.

When John Claypool was pastor of the Crescent Hill Baptist Church in Louisville, Kentucky, his 10-year-old daughter died of leukemia. Throughout that process, Claypool openly shared his deepest feelings, including his bewilderment and even his anger with God. The result was a deepened kinship between him and his congregation. And his sermons, which were later collected and published as a book called *Tracks of a Fellow Struggler,* have helped thousands of people deal with their own life struggles.[9]

Good preaching must be human. We must share some of the joy and pain of our own pilgrimage if we are to be authentic. Obviously, this can be overdone. I'm not advocating that we bear our souls every Sunday. Sometimes our own struggles must be left behind when we enter the pulpit. We should never overdo personal references. But occasionally, our people need to be reminded that we are real people. Expressing our humanity will make our preaching far more effective.

I have a sermon on this subject that I've preached at all three churches where I have served as pastor. It has helped introduce my humanity to my congregation. The title of the sermon is, "We Are Men Like Yourselves." The text is Acts 14:8-23 which tells about Paul's experience at Lystra.

The sermon revolves around two points—the person and the purpose of a pastor. I like to preach it early in my ministry at a new church. Although I've revised it a bit at each church, the basic thrust is the same.

The first half of the sermon deals with the pastor as a person. The focus is verse 15 where Paul said, "We also are men, of like nature with you." I want the congregation to know that I am a human being just like them.

I begin the sermon by telling about an incident in my first pastorate. Boxes were everywhere. The moving van had just left. In spite of my fatigue, I was bursting with excitement. This was my first pastorate out of seminary. I was young and I looked young, too.

About 10 o'clock the next morning the doorbell rang. A visitor dropped by the parsonage to meet the new pastor. He looked startled when I came to the door. He finally asked, "Is your father home?"

My visitor was confused. My youthfulness did not fit his image of a pastor. People often have inaccurate concepts about pastors and their families. This was certainly the case with the apostle Paul when he visited Lystra.

The people in this story made two mistakes concerning a minister of the gospel. The Greeks wanted to make gods of Paul and Barnabas. Unfortunately, people are still guilty of this mistake. They don't realize or accept the humanity of their pastor, and they put him on a pedestal. The problem with this is that sooner or later they will see his clay feet and be disappointed.

On the other hand, the Jews wanted to kill Paul and Barnabas. They stoned Paul and left him for dead. While the Greeks treated Paul as though he were more than a man, the Jews treated him as less than a man. Sadly, people today continue to mistreat ministers, often by cruel and vicious criticism.

Somewhere between making a god out of ministers and stoning them is the right perspective. Paul simply wanted to be treated like a human being. He cried out to the crowd, "We too are only men, human like you."

I tell my congregation that pastors are real people.

They can be noble and self-sacrificing; they can also be petty and intolerant. Preachers have dreams, hopes, and aspirations. They occasionally get bored or depressed. Although they love church work, sometimes they get discouraged and frustrated.

Pastors have feelings. They love their congregations but are often hurt by unrealistic expectations and unfair criticism. The pastorate is a demanding and difficult job. Your pastor appreciates your support and prayers. He is trying his best but is far from perfect. As Paul said, "We too are only men, human like you."

At this point I have a little fun in the sermon and tell several stories to illustrate my humanity. I then take a few minutes to illustrate the humanity of my wife and children. The last time I preached this sermon I told about a discussion between my wife and the pulpit committee a few months earlier.

We were in the middle of an interview. Things had been going extremely well. Late in the interview, however, one of the committee members asked my wife, "Paula, in your opinion, what is the role of a pastor's wife?"

I was nervous. Paula responded, "I think your question is a bit unfair." I almost had a heart attack!

She explained herself. "What I mean is that there is no one role for a pastor's wife. Each one is a unique individual and will have a different role."

I was proud of my wife's response. I was also greatly relieved when the committee responded favorably to her answer!

I then told a few brief stories about my children and how they were normal kids, just like anybody else's children. They can be sweet and adorable; they are also capable of mischief. Preacher's kids learn memory verses in Church Training but also beat up their sisters.

While this section of the sermon is humorous and fun, an important message is being communicated to my new congregation: Your preacher and his family are normal human beings.

The second half of the sermon deals with the purpose of the pastor, and I will not develop it here. Briefly, however, I tell them my philosophy of pastoral ministry. As I see it, the pastor has three primary duties—to proclaim the gospel, to lead the church, and to provide pastoral care to the people. I turn to various verses in the text to illustrate how Paul was involved in these same duties. I conclude the sermon by telling the people how glad I am to be their pastor and how much I look forward to working with them in the future.

The best sermon I ever heard on this subject was preached by Bill Leonard at the 1983 Christian Life Commission Seminar. The title of his sermon was "We Have This Treasure."

In this sermon Leonard traced the ministry of the apostle Paul. He noted Paul's brokenness, frailty, and weaknesses. And yet, in that earthen vessel, the great treasure of the gospel was being lived out. Leonard concluded his sermon in this way:

Today let us together confess with Paul what we really are . . . earthen vessels, weak, vulnerable, even broken, filled to overflowing with the treasure of the gospel.

So there he goes—hobbling down the road to Rome and the fulfillment of his destiny. "The apostle with the cauliflower ear and the split lip," someone has called him. Think of it! The good news of Jesus Christ is being carried to the world by a sickly, unimpressive, inarticulate Jew—how disgusting! Hallelujah![10]

Notes

1. Chevis R. Horne, "The Preacher and His Humanity," *The Baptist Program,* September 1984, 14-15.

2. William H. Willimon, *What's Right with the Church* (San Francisco: Harper and Row, 1985), 48.

3. Horne, 14.

4. Martin Buber, *Tales of the Hasidim: the Later Masters* (New York: Schocken books, 1948), 157.

5. Clyde E. Fant, *Preaching for Today* (San Francisco: Harper and Row, 1975), 184.

6. Buber, 199.

7. John Killinger, *Fundamentals of Preaching* (Philadelphia: Fortress Press, 1985), 157-58.

8. Cited in *The Christian Century,* May 11, 1988, Vol. 105, No. 16, p. 467, from David S. Reynold, *Beneath the American Renaissance* (Knopf, 1988), 23.

9. John Claypool, *Tracks of a Fellow Struggler* (Waco: Word, 1974).

10. From the 1983 Christian Life Commission Seminar Proceedings, published by the Christian Life Commission of the Southern Baptist Convention, Nashville, Tennessee.

Conclusion

Soon after completing this book I became the editor of *Proclaim,* a preaching and worship magazine at the Baptist Sunday School Board in Nashville, Tennessee. Although I'm enjoying my new position, I miss the pastorate, especially worship leadership and preaching. It is my hope and prayer, however, that God will use me in this new position to help pastors fulfill their worship leadership and preaching tasks.

One of the great responsibilities and joys of pastoral ministry is getting ready for Sunday. An important part of that process is getting ready for Sunday's sermon. For me, that means making an honest effort to preach sermons which are planned, relevant, engaging, authoritative, comprehensive, and human. As they say in my circles, "This will preach."